PIANO · VOCAL · GUITAR

GrandOleOpry®
CLASSIC LOVE SONGS

CLASSIC LOVE SONGS

ISBN 978-1-4234-5461-8

HAL•LEONARD®
CORPORATION
7777 W. BLUEMOUND RD. P.O. BOX 13819 MILWAUKEE, WI 53213

Visit Hal Leonard Online at
www.halleonard.com

CONTENTS

Look at Us
Opry Couples Backstage and Onstage

Connie Smith and
Marty Stuart
Chris Hollo

Eddy Arnold
and family

Trisha Yearwood
and Garth Brooks
Donnie Beauchamp

George Jones
and Tammy Wynette
Les Leverett

June and Johnny Cash
Les Leverett

Henry and
Sarah Cannon
Bill Goodman

Ricky Skaggs and Sharon White
Les Leverett

Amy Grant and Vince Gill
Chris Hollo

Wilma Lee, Stoney and Carol Lee Cooper
Gordon Gillingham

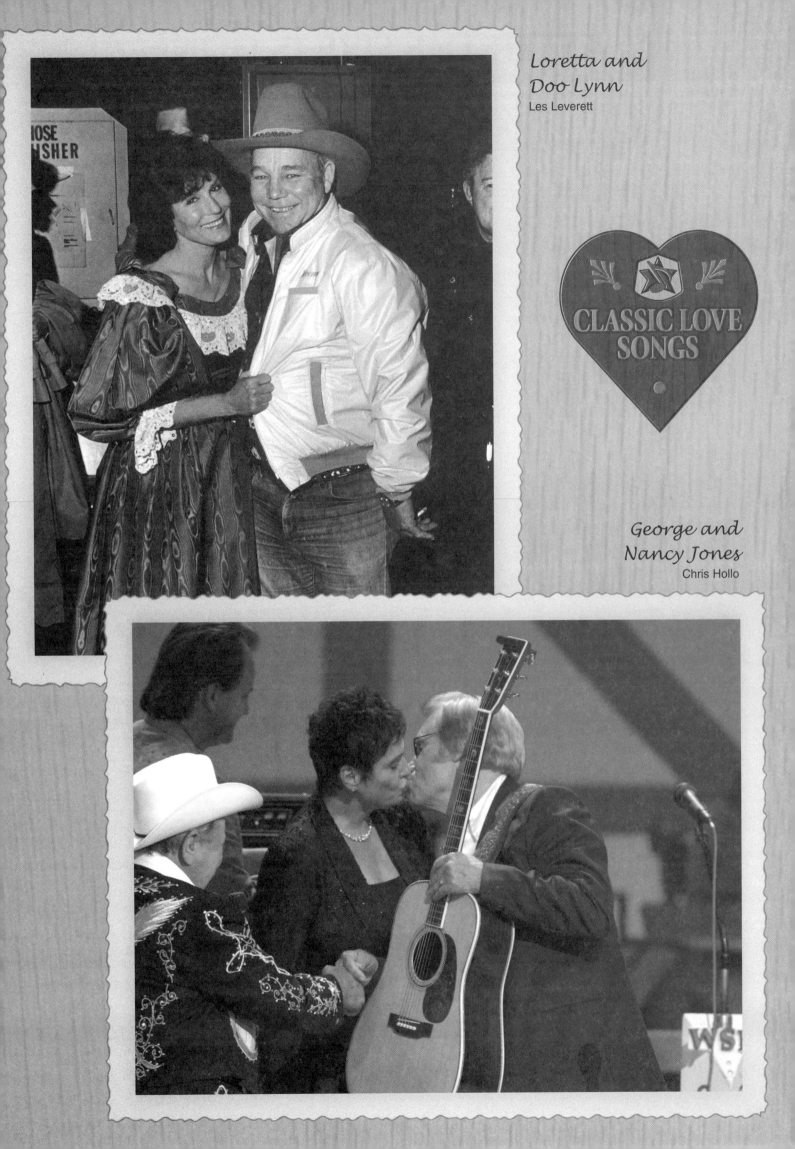

Loretta and
Doo Lynn
Les Leverett

CLASSIC LOVE
SONGS

George and
Nancy Jones
Chris Hollo

AFTER THE FIRE IS GONE

Words and Music by
L.E. WHITE

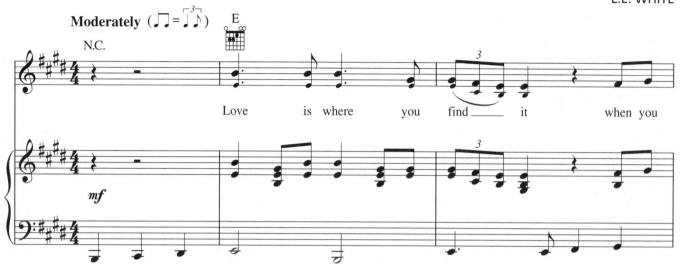

Love is where you find _____ it when you

find _____ no love at home. And there's noth-in' cold _____ as

ash - es _____ af - ter the fire _____ is gone.

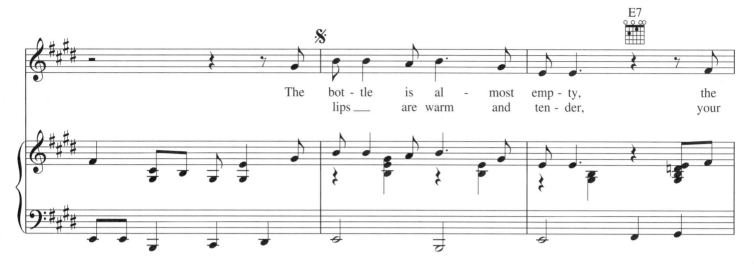

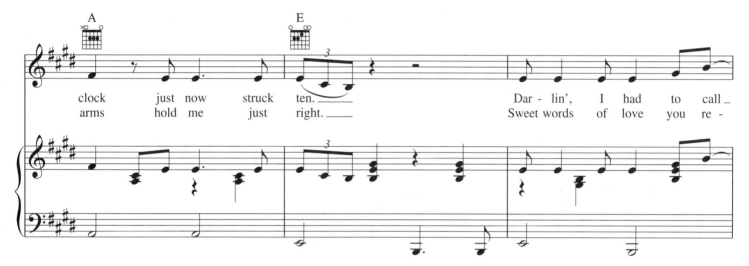

home. ____
on. ____

And there's noth - in' cold ____ as ash - es ____

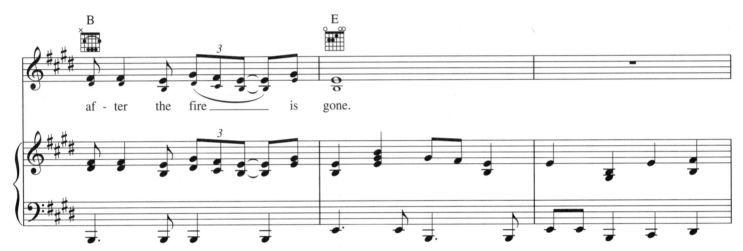

af - ter the fire ____ is gone.

Love is where you find ____ it when you find ____ no love at

home. And there's noth - in' cold ____ as ash - es ____

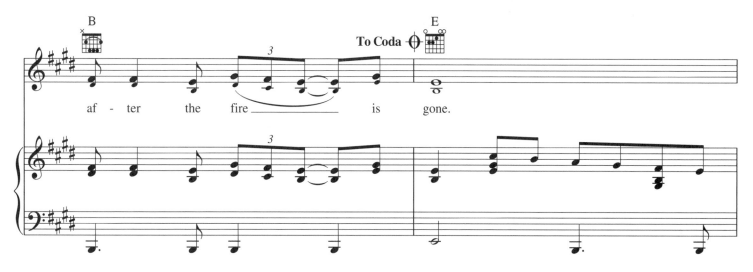

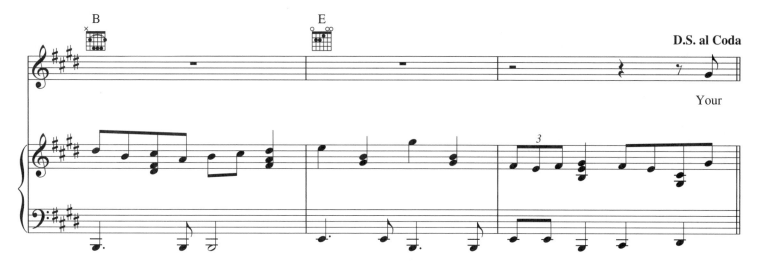

ALL I HAVE TO DO IS DREAM

Words and Music by
BOUDLEAUX BRYANT

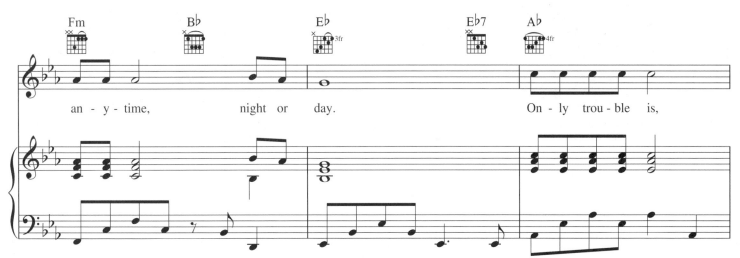

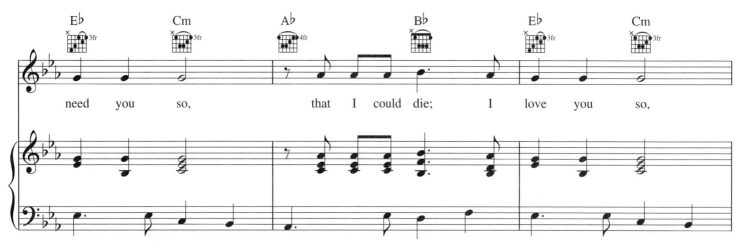

need you so, that I could die; I love you so,

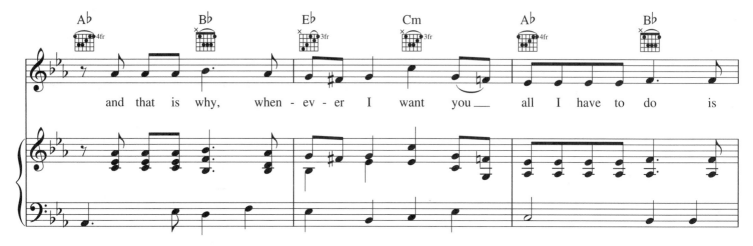

and that is why, when-ev-er I want you ___ all I have to do is

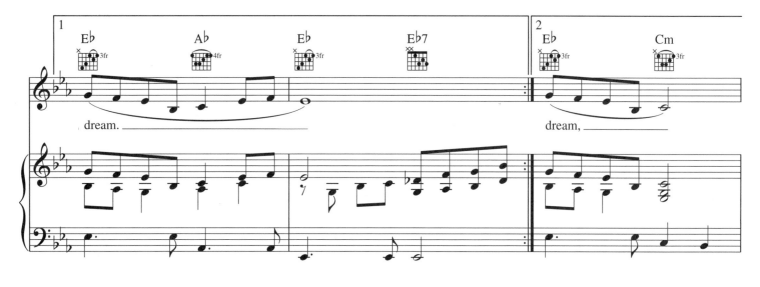

dream. ___ dream, ___

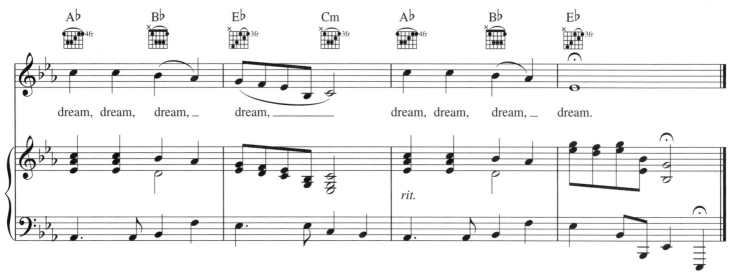

dream, dream, dream, _ dream, ___ dream, dream, dream, _ dream.

ALWAYS LATE WITH YOUR KISSES

Words and Music by BLACKIE CRAWFORD
and LEFTY FRIZZELL

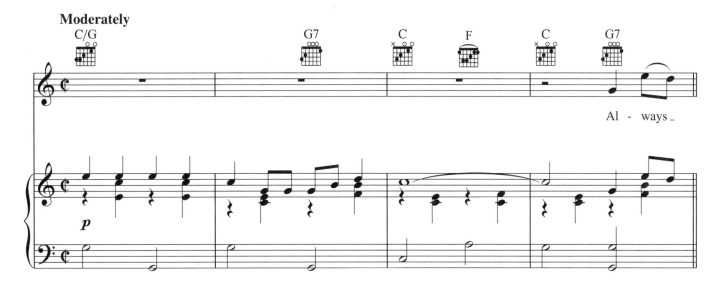

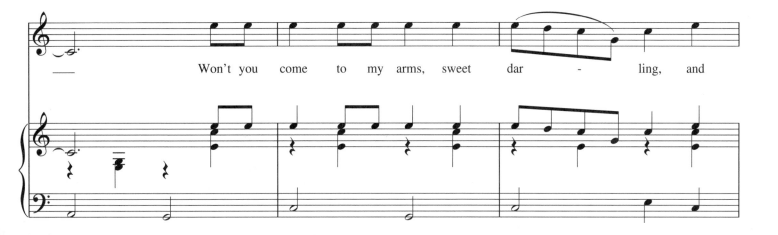

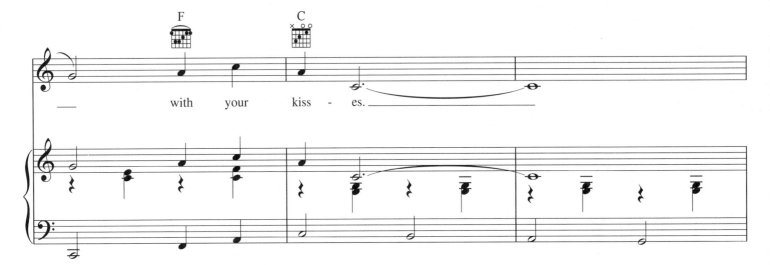

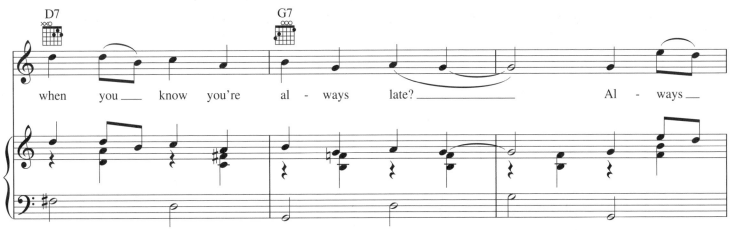

when you ___ know you're al - ways late? _____ Al - ways ___

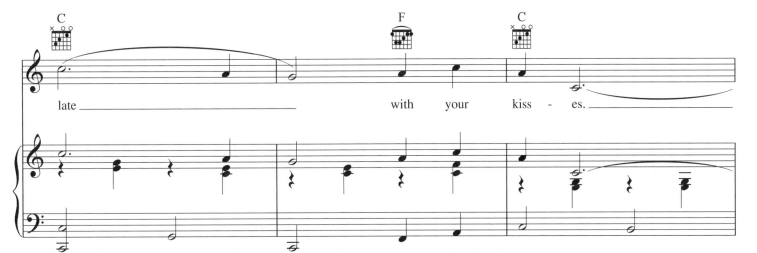

late _____ with your kiss - es. _____

Why, oh, why do you want to do me this

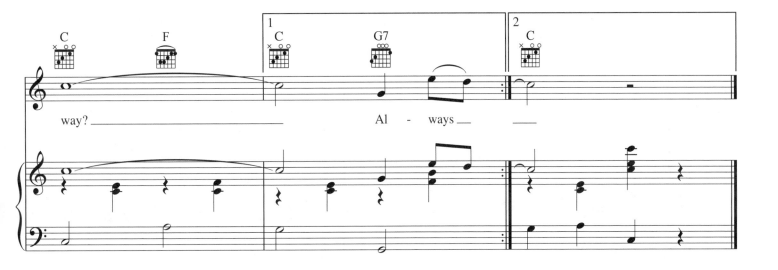

way? _____ Al - ways ___ ___

ALWAYS ON MY MIND

Words and Music by WAYNE THOMPSON,
MARK JAMES and JOHNNY CHRISTOPHER

May-be I did-n't treat you ___ quite as good ___ as I
May-be I did-n't hold you ___ all those lone-ly, lone-ly

should have.
times, ___ and I guess I nev-er told you ___ May-be I did-n't love you ___

quite as of-ten as I could have. ___ (1.,3.) Lit-tle things I should have
I'm so hap-py that you're mine. _____ (2.) If I made you feel ___

me, give me one more chance to keep you sat - is - fied, sat - is -

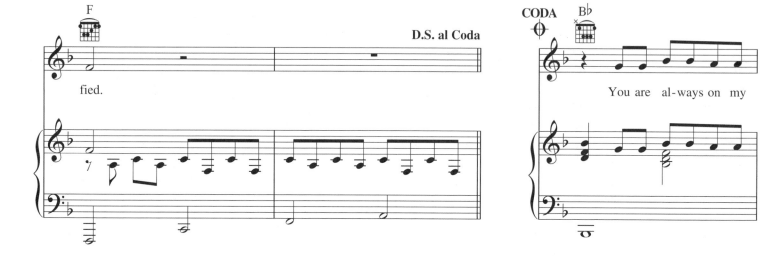

D.S. al Coda **CODA**

fied. You are al - ways on my

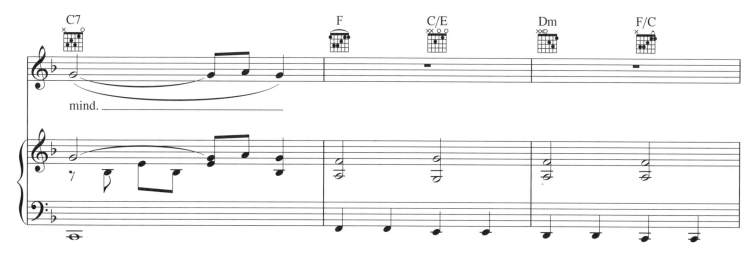

mind. _____

You are al - ways on my mind.

rit.

ANYMORE

Words and Music by TRAVIS TRITT
and JILL COLUCCI

out of my eyes __ an - y - more. _____
- dle an - y - where _ next to you. _____

My tears no long - er wait -
My heart can't take the beat -

- ing. __ My re - sist - ance ain't _ that strong. _
- ing __ not _ hav - ing you _ to hold. _

My mind keeps re - cre - at - ing __ a love with you _ a - lone. _
A small voice keeps re - peat - ing __ deep in - side _ my soul. _

And I'm tired of pre - tend - ing ___
It says I can't keep pre - tend - ing ___

I don't love you an - y - more. ___
I don't love you an - y - more.

Let me make ___

I've got to take ___ the chance ___ or ___ let it pass by ___

if I ex - pect to get on ___ with my life. ___

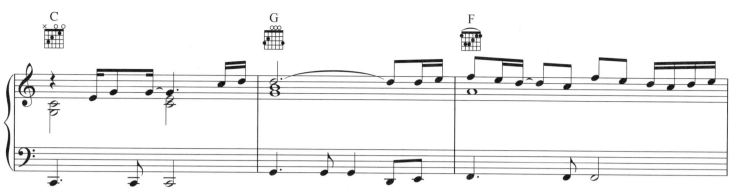

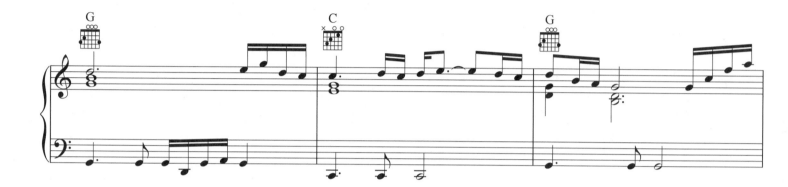

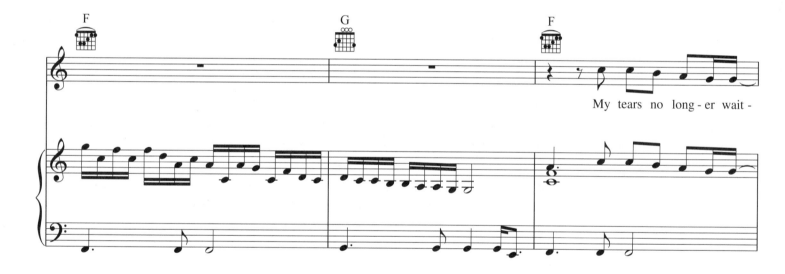

My tears no long-er wait-

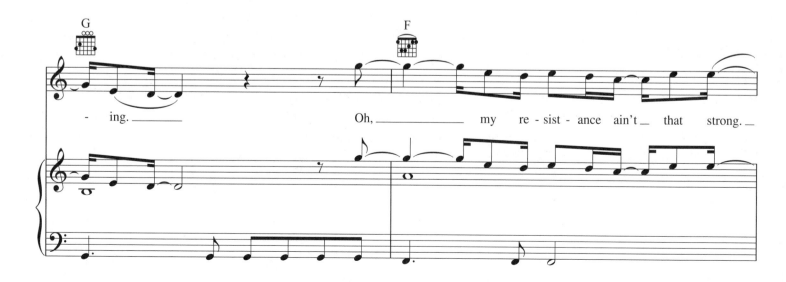

-ing. _____ Oh, _____ my re-sist-ance ain't_ that strong._

ANGEL FLYING TOO CLOSE TO THE GROUND

Words and Music by
WILLIE NELSON

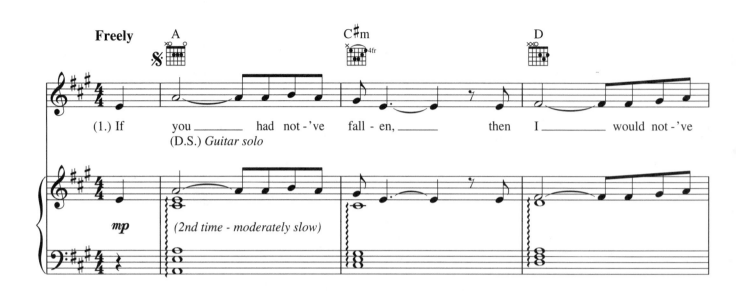

(1.) If you _____ had not -'ve fall - en, _____ then I _____ would not -'ve
(D.S.) *Guitar solo*

mp (2nd time - moderately slow)

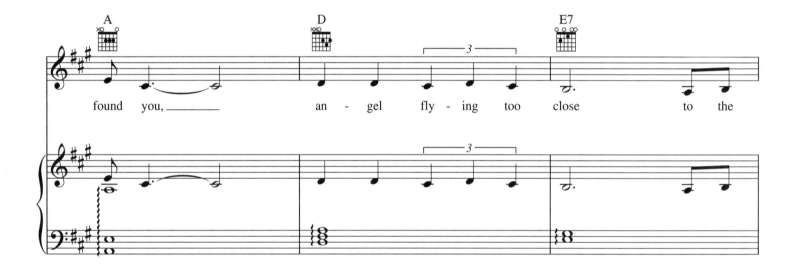

found you, _____ an - gel fly - ing too close to the

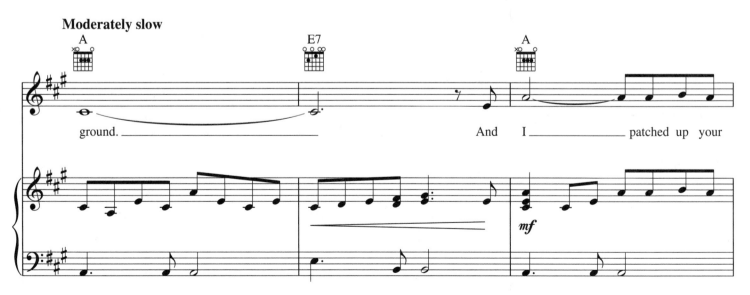

ground. _____ And I _____ patched up your

mf

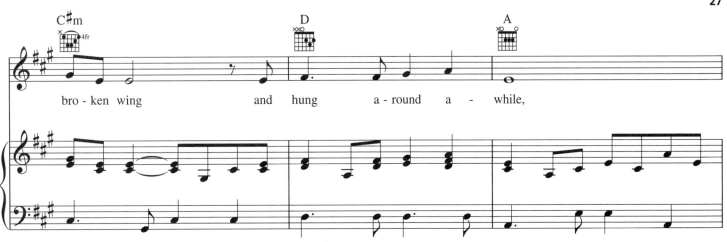

bro - ken wing and hung a - round a - while,

try - ing to keep your spir - its up and your

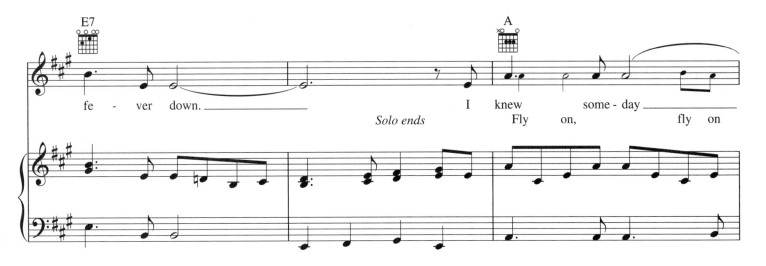

fe - ver down. _____ *Solo ends* I knew some - day _____ Fly on, fly on

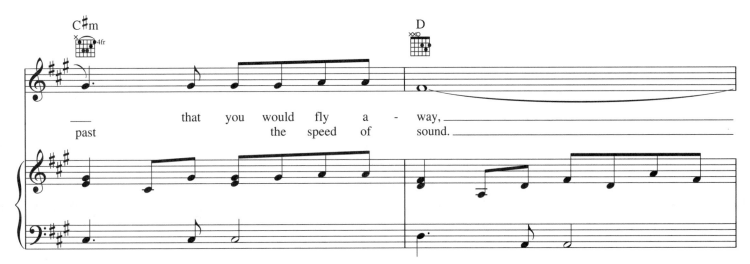

_____ that you would fly a - way, _____
past the speed of sound. _____

for love's the great-est heal-er to be
I'd rath-er see you up____ than see you

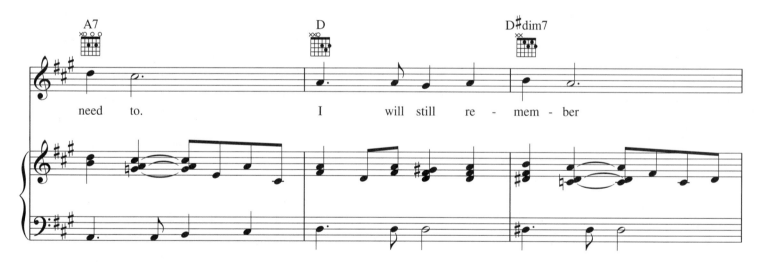

found._____ So leave me if you
down._____ So

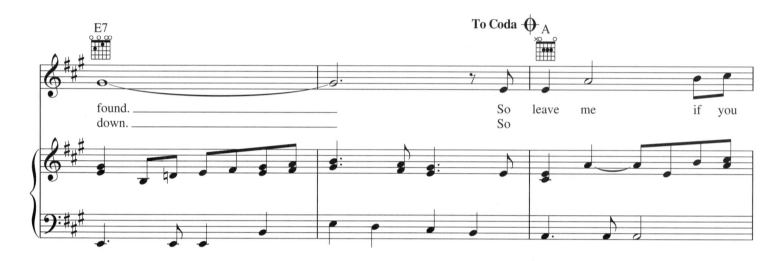

need to. I will still re-mem-ber

an-gel fly-ing too close to the ground._____

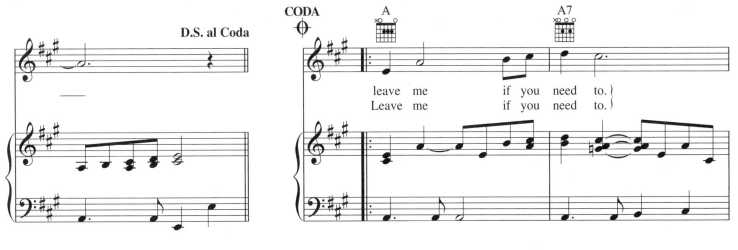

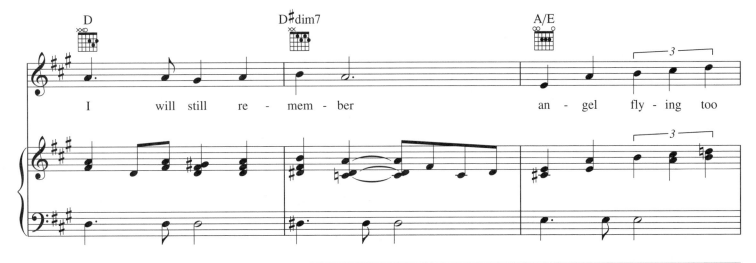

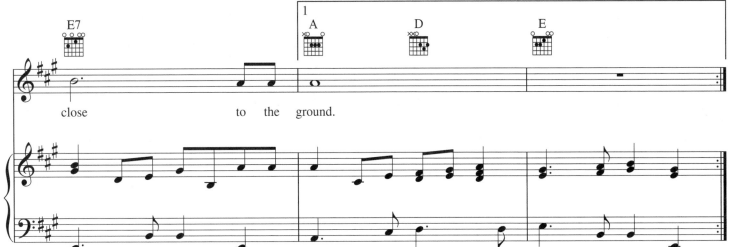

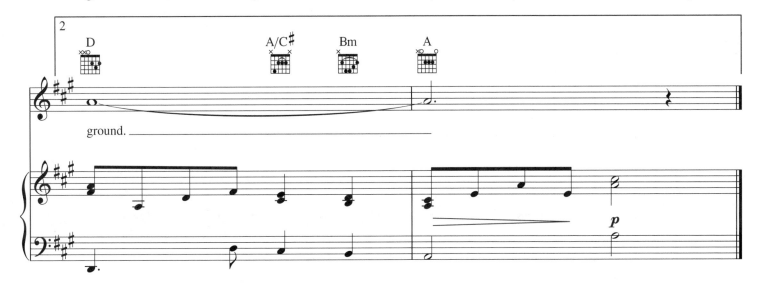

BEAUTIFUL MESS

Words and Music by SONNY LeMAIRE,
CLAY MILLS and SHANE MINOR

Go - in' out of my mind these days. ___

Like I'm walk - in' 'round in a haze. ___

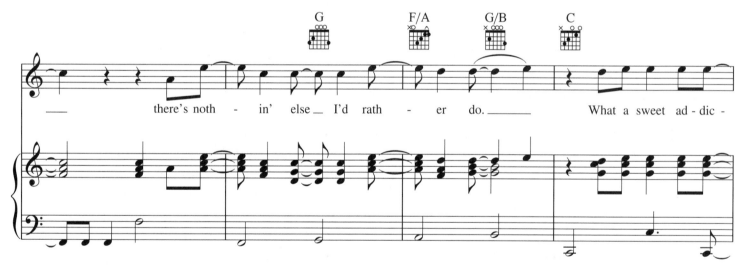

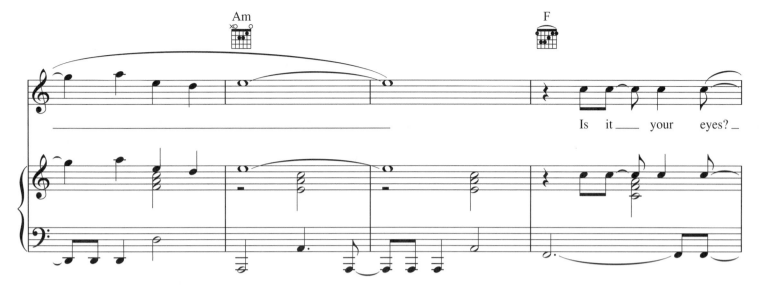

Is it ___ your eyes? ___

Is it ___ your smile? ___ All I

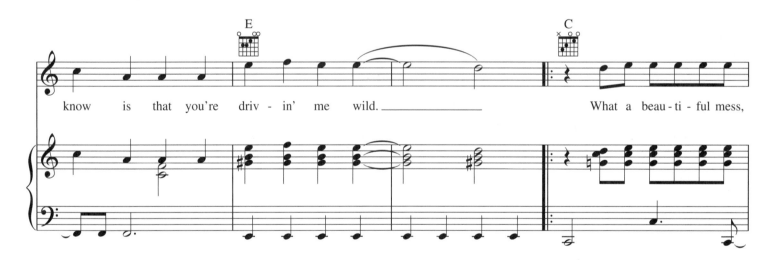

know is that you're driv-in' me wild. ___ What a beau-ti-ful mess,

what a beau-ti-ful mess ___ I'm in. ___ Spend-in' all ___ my time ___ with you, ___

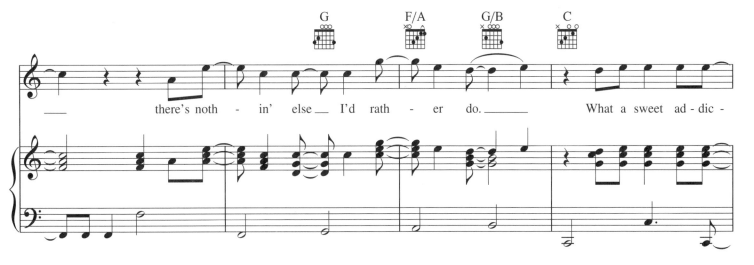

there's noth - in' else __ I'd rath - er do. _____ What a sweet ad - dic -

- tion that I'm caught __ up in. _____ 'Cause I ____ can't get __ e - nough, __

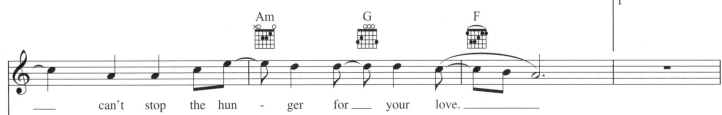

____ can't stop the hun - ger for __ your love. _____

What a beau - ti - ful, ____ what a beau - ti - ful mess __ I'm in ____

BLUE EYES CRYING IN THE RAIN

Words and Music by
FRED ROSE

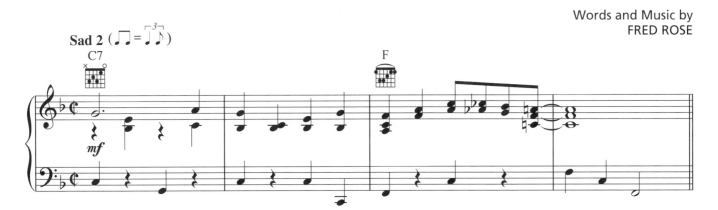

In the twi-light glow I see her,
Now my hair has turned to sil - ver.

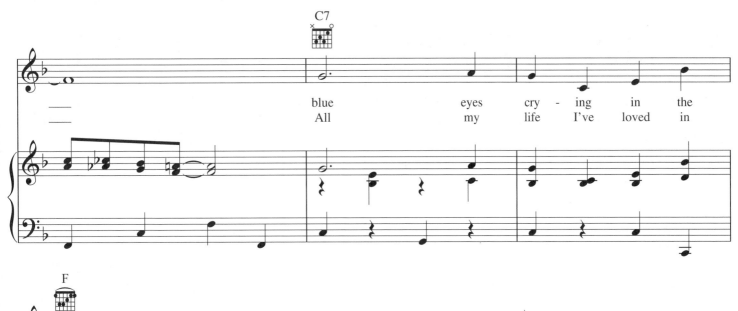

blue eyes cry-ing in the
All my life I've loved in

rain.
vain.

As we
I can

kissed good - bye and part - ed,_____ I
see her star in heav - en,_____

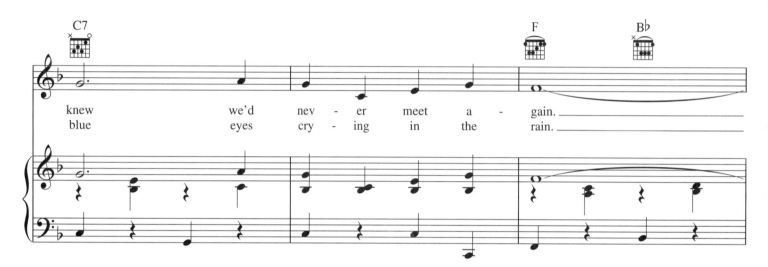

knew we'd nev - er meet a - gain._____
blue eyes cry - ing in the rain._____

Love is like a dy - ing
Some - day when we meet up

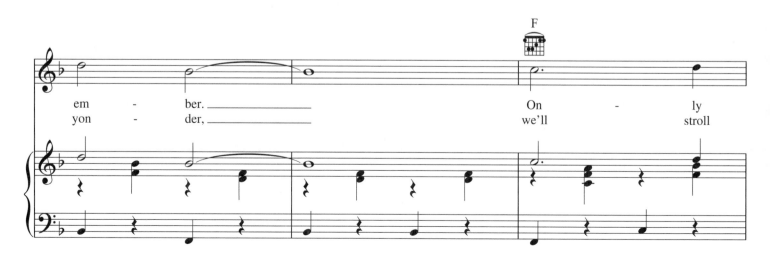

em - ber._____ On - ly
yon - der,_____ we'll stroll

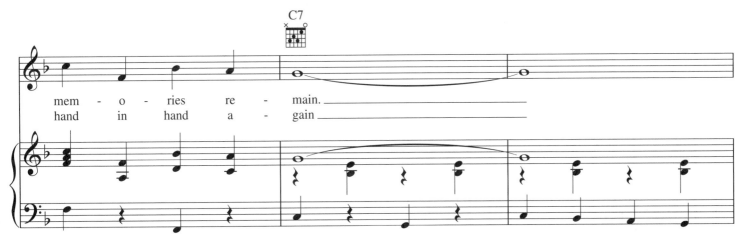

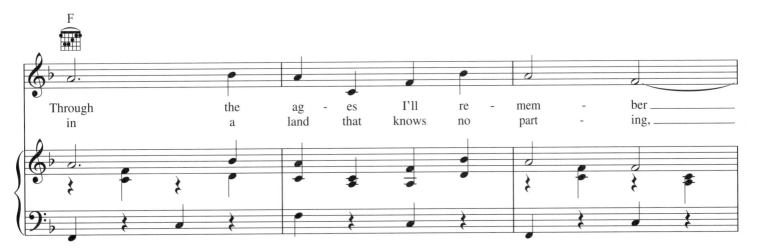

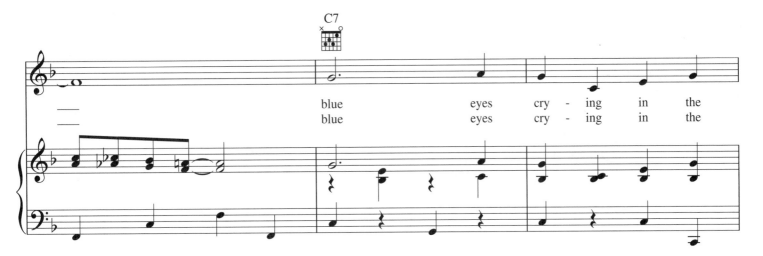

BORN TO LOSE

Words and Music by
TED DAFFAN

Moderately

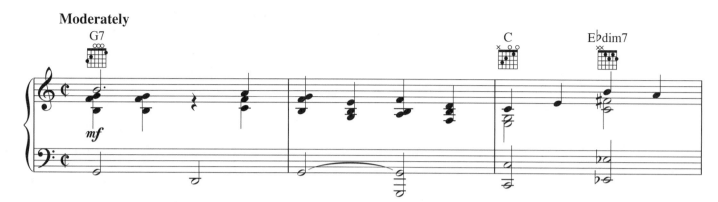

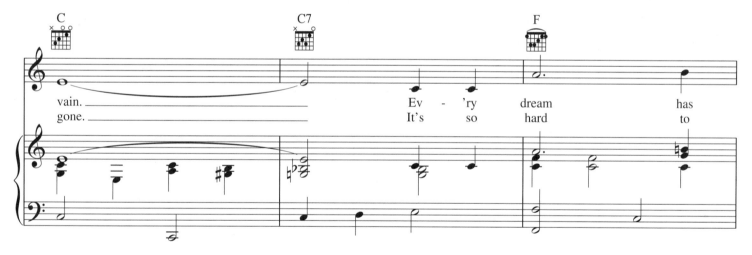

Born to lose, I've lived my life in
lose, my ev - 'ry hope is

vain. _____
gone. _____

Ev - 'ry dream has
It's so hard to

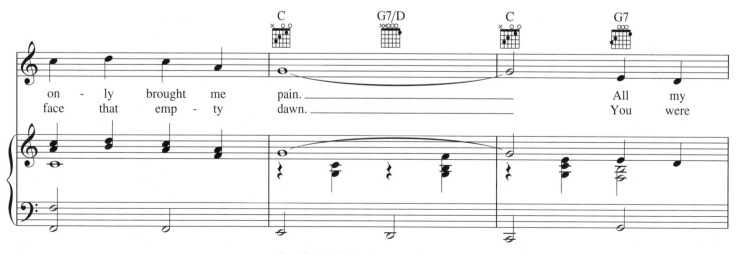

on - ly brought me pain. _____ All my
face that emp - ty dawn. _____ You were

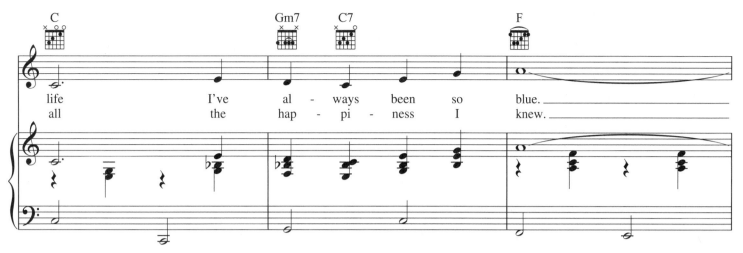

life   I've   al - ways   been   so   blue.

all   the   hap - pi - ness   I   knew.

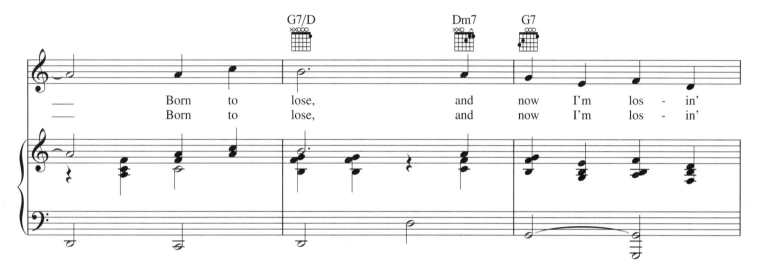

Born   to   lose,   and   now   I'm   los - in'

Born   to   lose,   and   now   I'm   los - in'

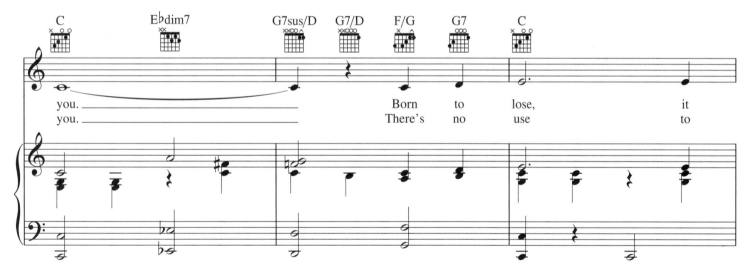

you.   Born   to   lose,   it

you.   There's   no   use   to

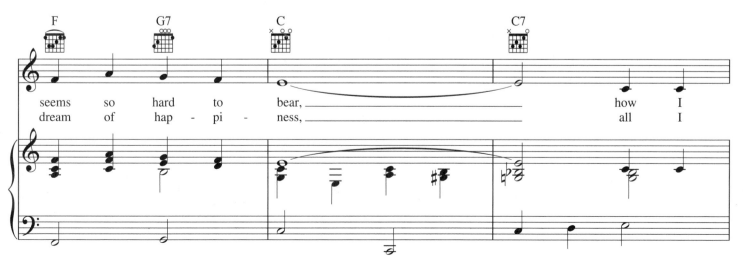

seems   so   hard   to   bear,   how   I

dream   of   hap - pi - ness,   all   I

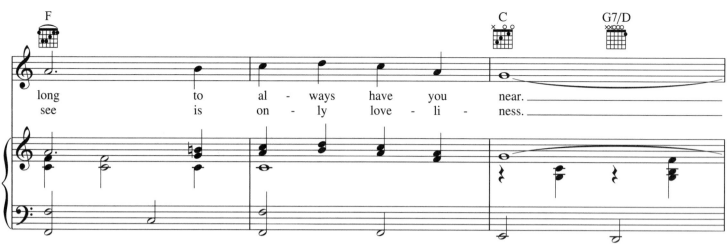

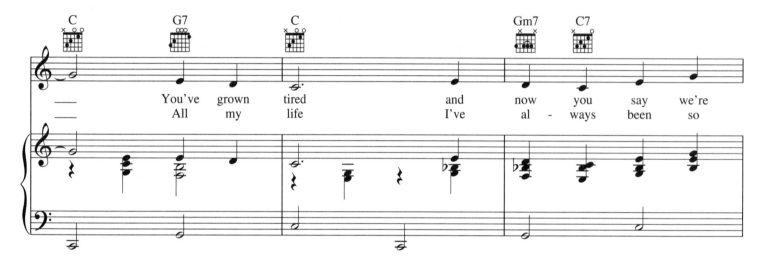

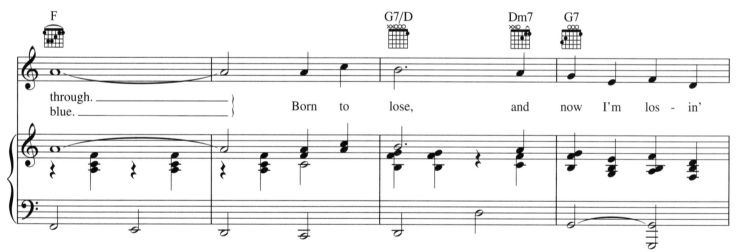

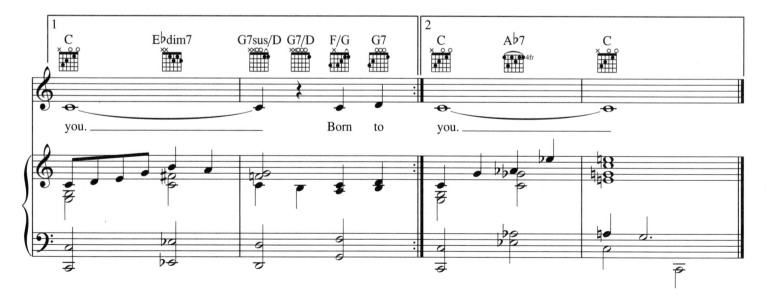

COLD, COLD HEART

Words and Music by
HANK WILLIAMS

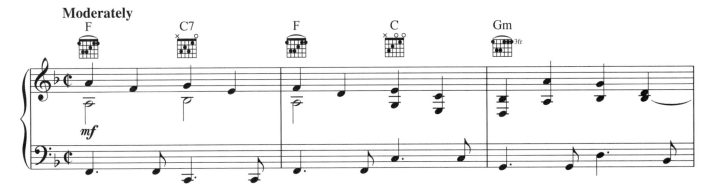

I tried so hard, my dear, to show that
nev-er know how much it hurts to

you're my ev-'ry dream, yet you're a-fraid each
see you sit and cry. You know you need each and

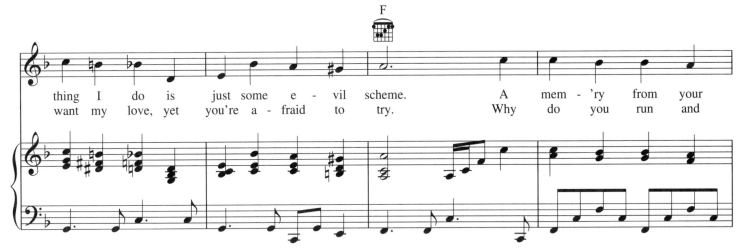

thing I do is just some e-vil scheme. A mem-'ry from your
want my love, yet you're a-fraid to try. Why do you run and

lone - some past keeps us so far a - part. Why
hide from past life? To us try it just ain't smart. Why

can't I free your doubt - ful mind and melt your cold, cold
can't I free your doubt - ful mind and melt your cold, cold

heart? An - oth - er love be - fore my time made your heart sad and
heart? There was a time when I be - lieved that you be - longed to

blue, and so my heart is pay - ing now for
me, but so now I know your heart is shack - led

COME A LITTLE CLOSER

Words and Music by DIERKS BENTLEY
and BRETT BEAVERS

If there's still _ a chance, _ then take _ my hand _ and we'll

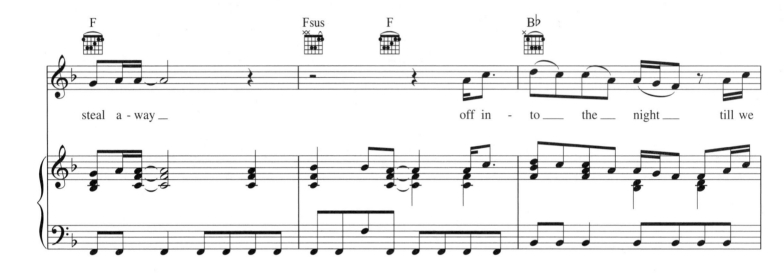

steal a - way _ off in - to _ the _ night _ till we

make _ things _ right. _ The sun's gon-na rise on a bet-ter day. _____

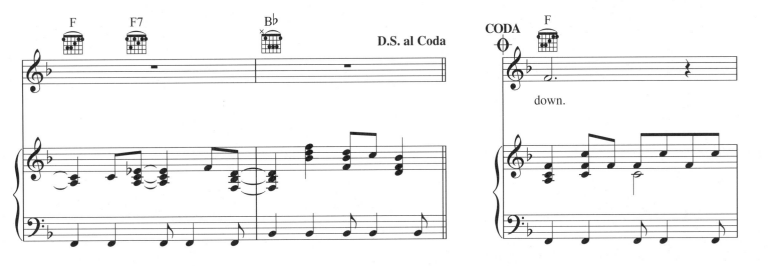

D.S. al Coda

CODA

down.

Come a lit-tle clos-er, ba — by,

just a lit-tle bit clos-er, ba — by.

Come a lit-tle clos-er, ba — by, I feel like lay-in' you down.

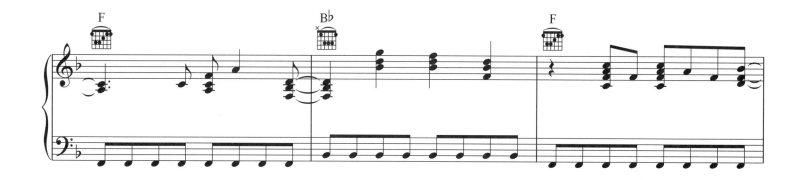

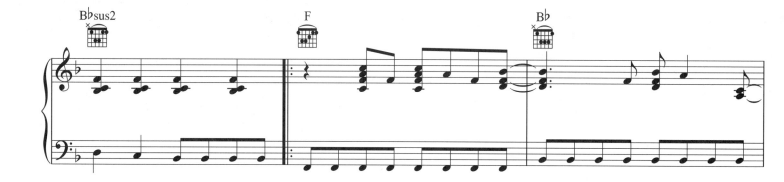

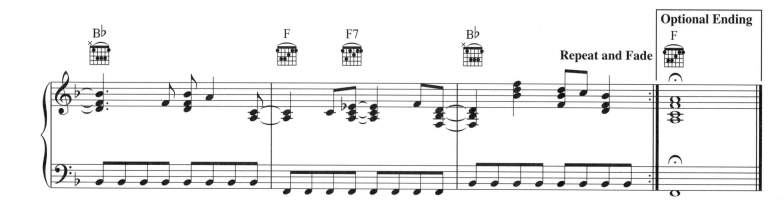

Optional Ending

Repeat and Fade

CRAZY

Words and Music by
WILLIE NELSON

Moderately slow

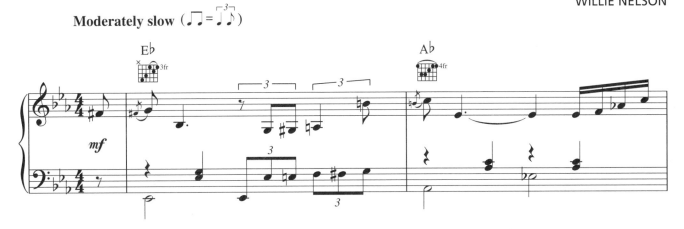

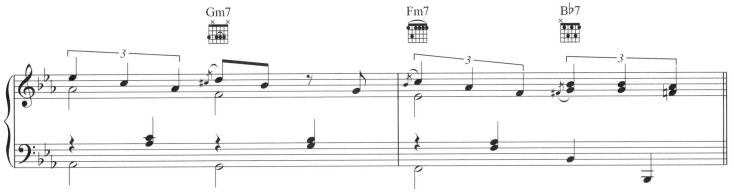

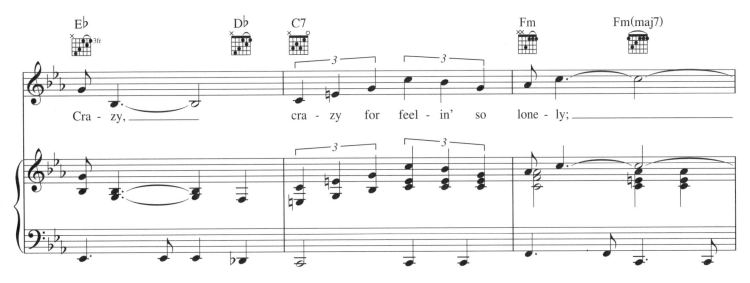

Cra - zy, _____ cra - zy for feel - in' so lone - ly; _____

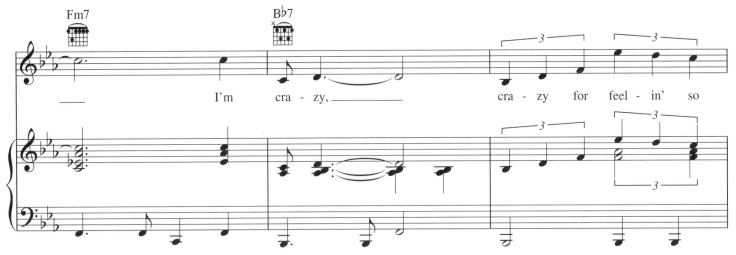

I'm cra - zy, _____ cra - zy for feel - in' so

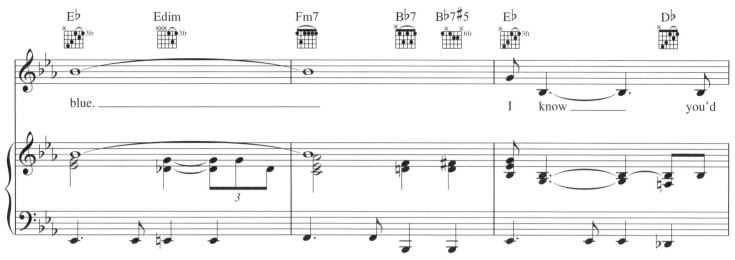

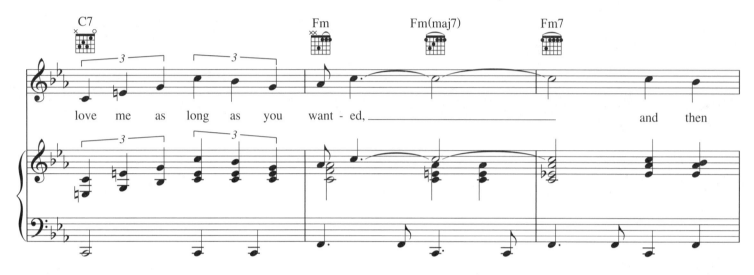

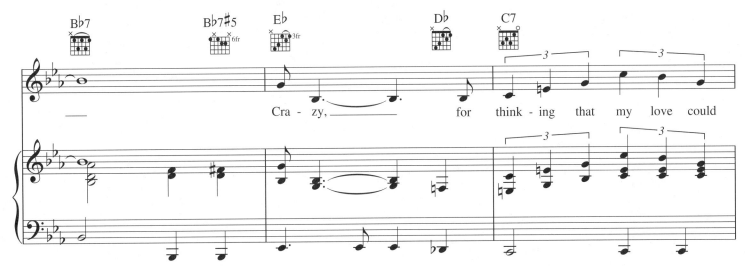

CRAZY ARMS

Words and Music by RALPH MOONEY
and CHARLES SEALS

mine. _____ }
time. _____ }
Cra - zy arms that reach to hold some-bod-y new, but my yearn-ing heart keeps say - ing you're not mine. _____ My trou-bled mind knows soon to an - oth - er you'll be wed, and that's why I'm lone - ly all the time. _____ time. _____

DEAR ME

Words and Music by JAMES CARSON WHITSETT
and SCOTT MATEER

Dear me, ___ oh, what have I done? ___ Oh, and dear me, ___ he's my

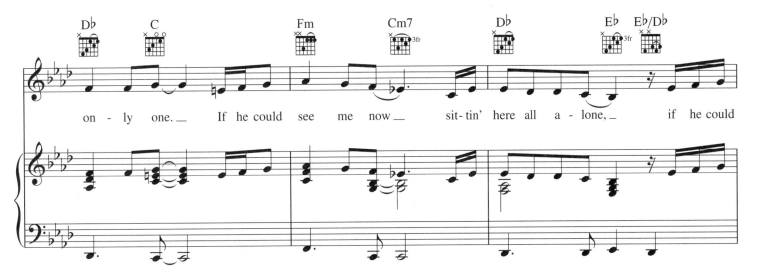

on - ly one. ___ If he could see me now ___ sit-tin' here all a - lone, ___ if he could

read these words, ___ would he come back home? ___ Dear

me.   2. Dear me.

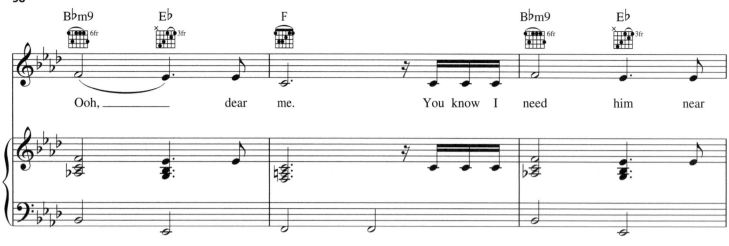

Ooh, _____ dear me. You know I need him near

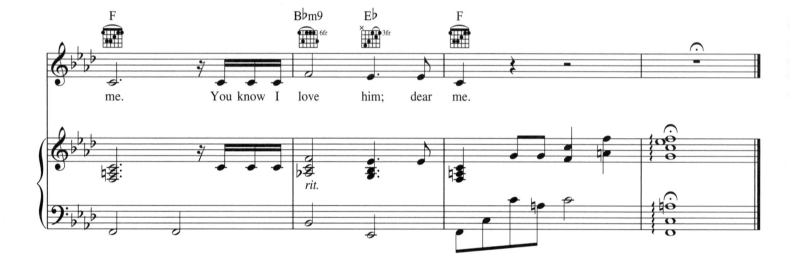

me. You know I love him; dear me.

Additional Lyrics

2. Dear me,
   Do you really mind?
   You're the only friend
   Who will take the time
   To hear me.
   Oh, and all the plans we've made,
   If he'll take me back,
   I'll do anything to make him stay.

   Dear me,
   We'll start all over again,
   Oh, and near me
   I hope he'll stay till the end.
   If he could see me now
   Sittin' here all alone,
   If he could read these words,
   Would he run back home?
   Dear me.

THE END OF THE WORLD

Words by SYLVIA DEE
Music by ARTHUR KENT

Melancholy Ballad

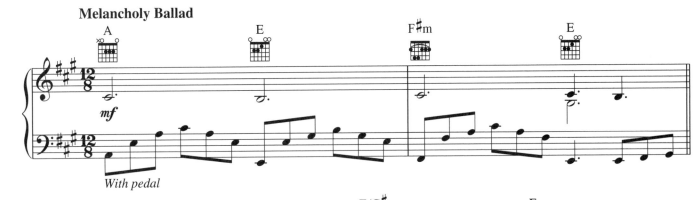

With pedal

Why _____ does the sun _____ go on _____ shin - ing? _____

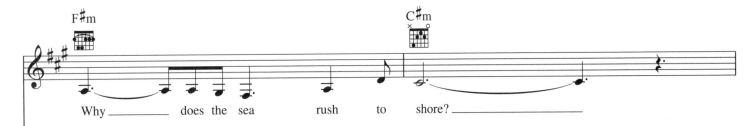

Why _____ does the sea _____ rush to shore? _____

Don't they _____ know _____ it's the end _____ of the world, _____ 'cause

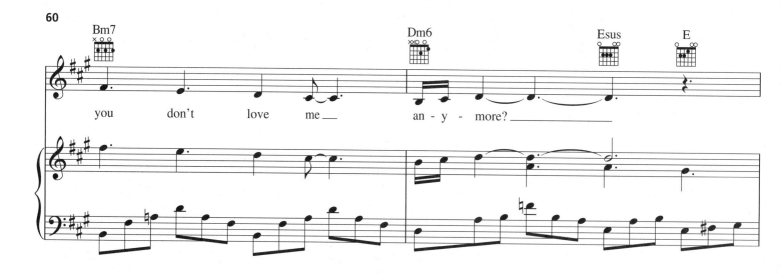

you don't love me ___ an-y-more? _____

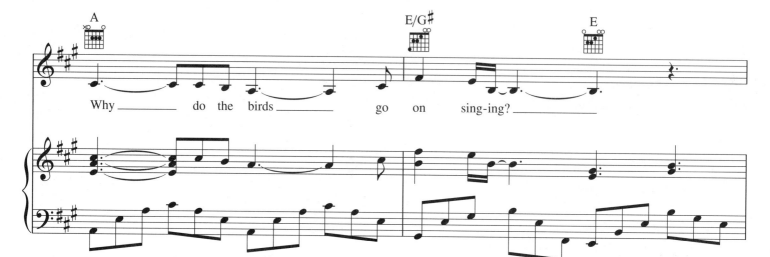

Why _____ do the birds _____ go on sing-ing? _____

Why _____ do the stars glow a - bove? _____

Don't they ___ know _____ it's the end _____ of the world? __ It

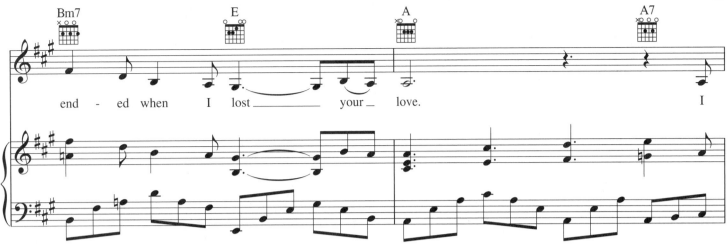

end - ed when I lost _____ your ___ love. I

wake up in the morn - ing and I _____ won - der _____ why ___

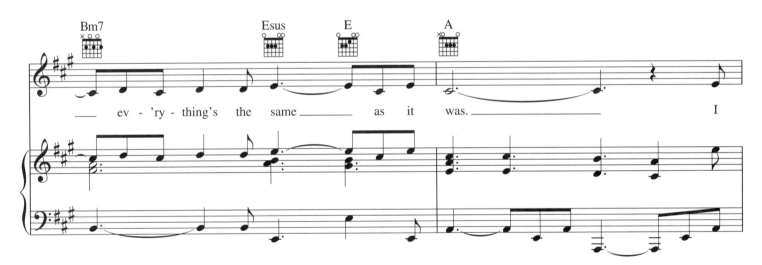

___ ev - 'ry - thing's the same _____ as it was. _____ I

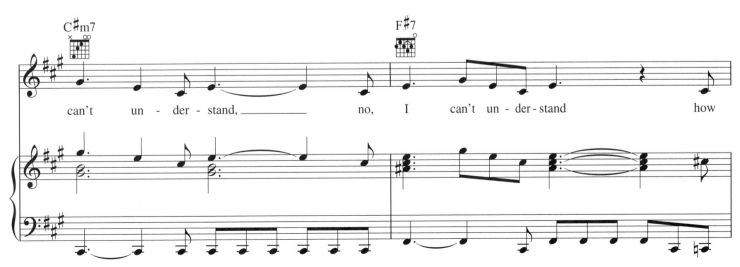

can't un - der - stand, _____ no, I can't un - der - stand how

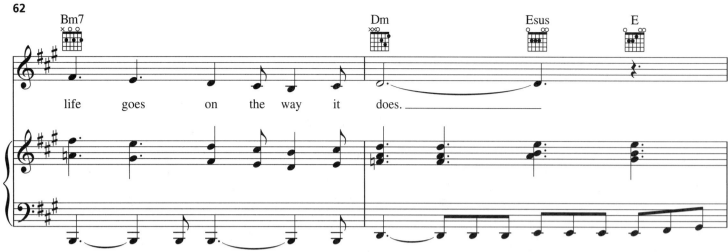

life goes on the way it does. _____

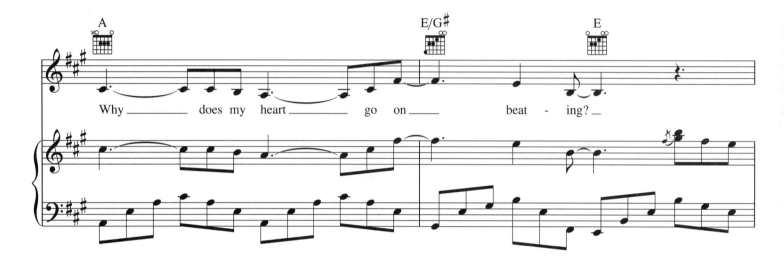

Why _____ does my heart _____ go on _____ beat - ing? ___

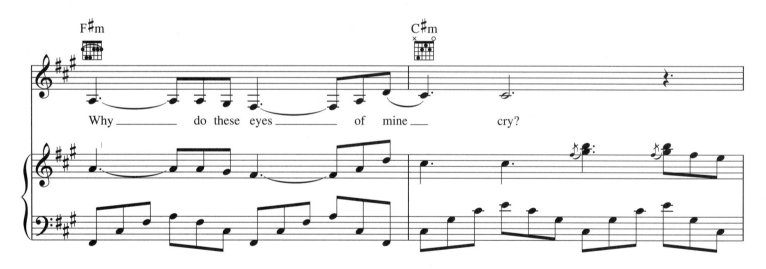

Why _____ do these eyes _____ of mine ___ cry?

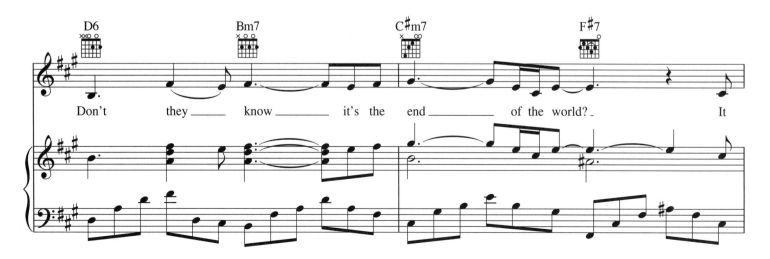

Don't they _____ know _____ it's the end _____ of the world? _ It

end - ed when you said _____ good - bye. _____

Don't they _____ know _____ it's the end _____ of the world? _____ It

end - ed when you _ said good - bye. _____

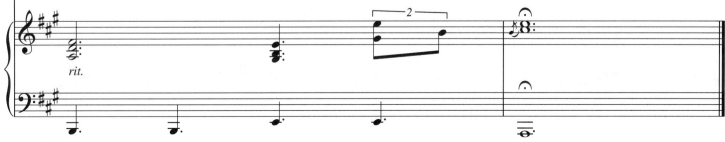

DEVIL WOMAN

Words and Music by
MARTY ROBBINS

1. I told Mar - y a - bout us, told her a - bout_ our great sin.
2.-4. *(See additional lyrics)*

Mar - y just cried and for - gave me; Mar - y took me back a - gain.___ She

said if I want - ed my free - dom I could be free_ ev - er - more.___ But

Additional Lyrics

2. Mary is waiting and weeping alone in our shack by the sea.
   Even after I hurt her, Mary's still in love with me.
   Devil woman, it's over. Trapped no more by your charms.
   I don't want to stay; I want to get away. Woman let go of my arms.
   Chorus

3. Devil woman, you're evil like the dark corral reef.
   Like the winds that bring high tides, you bring sorrow and grief.
   You made me ashamed to face Mary, barely had the strength to tell.
   Skies are not so black, Mary took me back. Mary has broken your spell.
   Chorus

4. Running alone by the seashore, running as fast as I can.
   Even the sea gulls are happy, glad I'm coming home again.
   Never again will I ever cause another tear to fall.
   Down the beach I see what belongs to me, the one I want most of all.
   Chorus

   Last Chorus:
   Devil woman, devil woman, don't follow me.
   Devil woman, let me be. Just leave me alone; I want to go home.

EVERY LIGHT IN THE HOUSE

Words and Music by
KENT ROBBINS

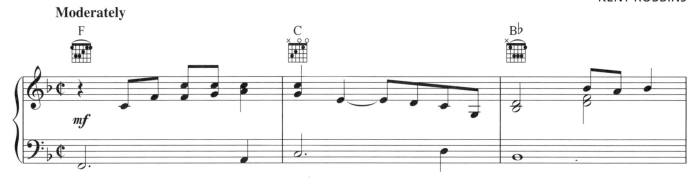

Moderately

I told you ___ I'd leave ___ the light ___ on ___ in
-er start ___ for - get - tin', I'll

case you ev - er want - ed to come ___ back home. ___ You smiled and said ___ you ap -
turn ___ the lights ___ off ___ one ___ by one, ___ so you can see ___ that ___

pre - ci - ate ___ the ges - ture.
I a - gree ___ it's o - ver. But un -
I

took your ev - 'ry word __ to heart ____ 'cause I can't stand __ us ____
til then I ____ want you ____ to know ____ if you look south, _ you'll _

be - in' a - part. __ And just to show how __ much __ I real - ly miss __
see __ a glow. _ That's me __ wait - in' at home __ each night _____ to

__ ya, }
hold ya. }
Ev - er - y light _____ in the

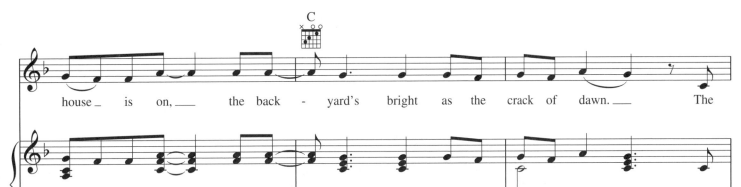

house _ is on, ___ the back - yard's bright as the crack of dawn. __ The

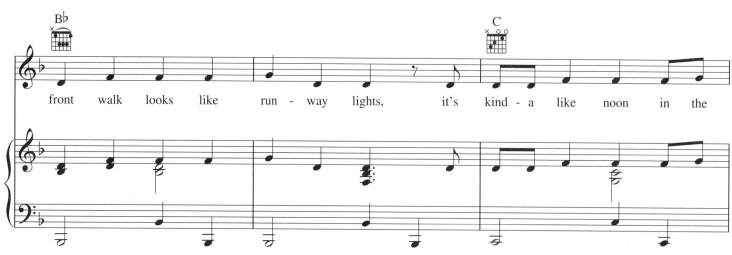

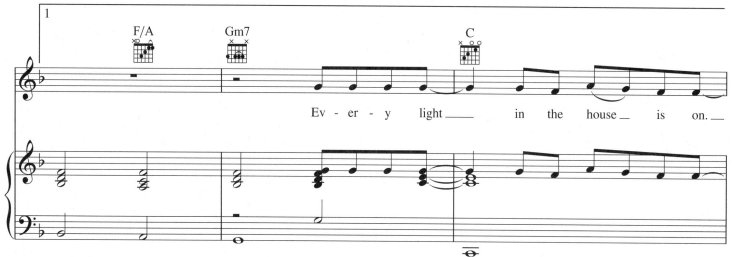

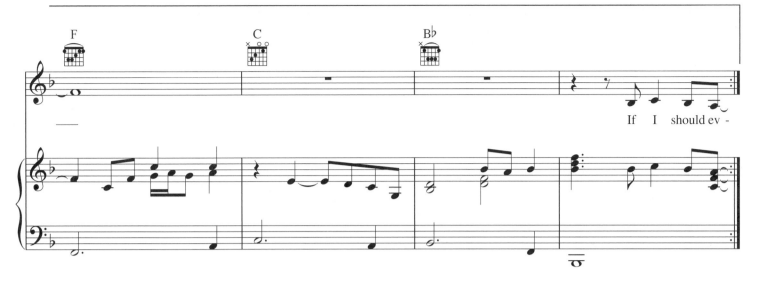

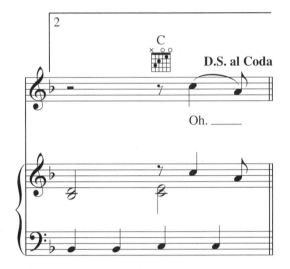

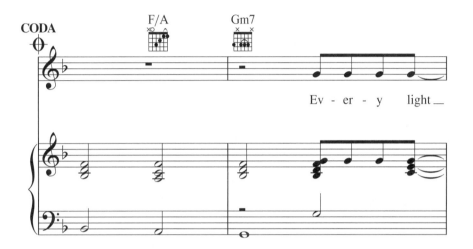

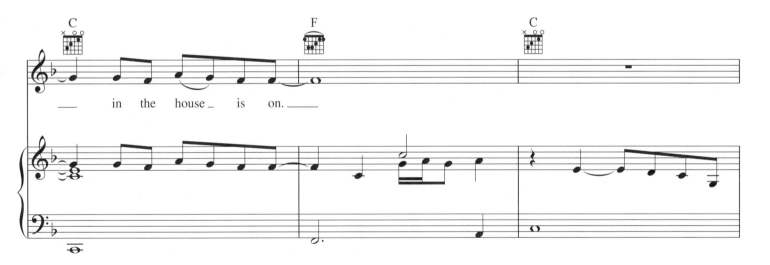

FOR THE GOOD TIMES

Words and Music by
KRIS KRISTOFFERSON

Slowly

Don't look so sad; _____ I know it's
long, _____ you'll find an-

o-ver, _____ but life goes on _____ and this old
oth-er, _____ and I'll be here _____ if you should

world _____ will keep on turn-ing. Let's just be
find _____ you ev-er need me. Don't say a

FOREVER AND EVER, AMEN

Words and Music by PAUL OVERSTREET
and DON SCHLITZ

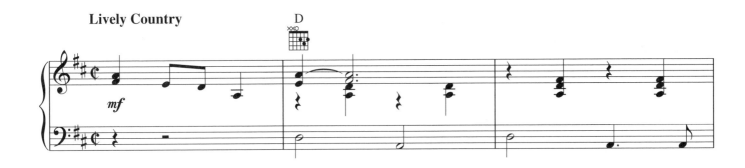

You may think that I'm ___
time takes its toll ___

___ talk - in' fool - ish.
___ on a bod - y,

You've
makes a

heard that I'm wild ___ and I'm free. ___
young girl's ___ brown ___ hair ___ turn gray.

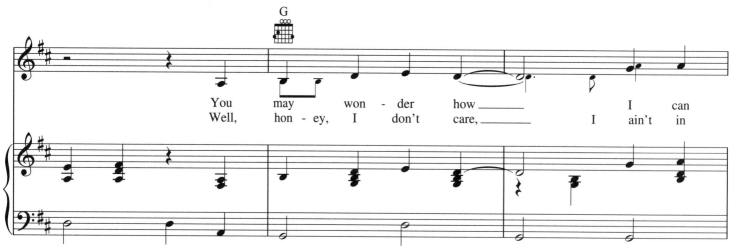

You may won - der how _____ I can
Well, hon - ey, I don't care, _____ I ain't in

prom - ise you now _____ and if this love that I feel _____
love with your hair, _____ and if it all _____ I fell out, _____

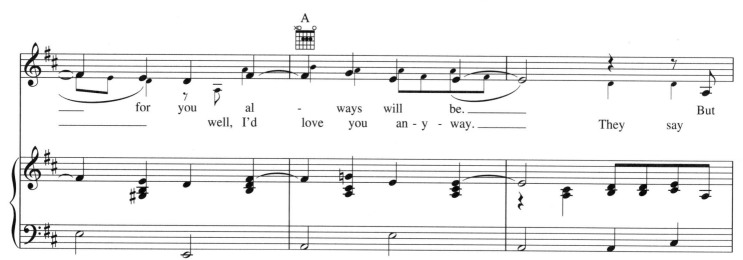

_____ for you al - ways will be. _____ But
well, I'd love you an - y - way. _____ They say

you're not just time _____ that I'm kill - in'.
time can just play tricks _____ on a mem - 'ry,

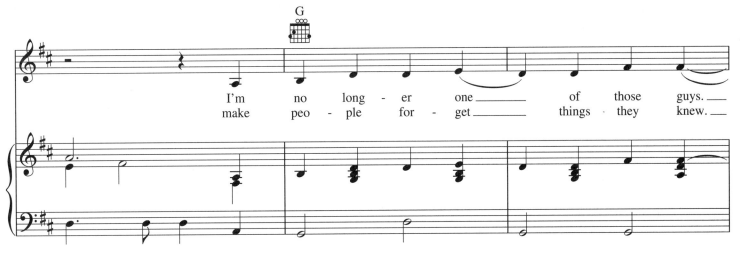

I'm no long - er one _____ of those guys. _____
make peo - ple for - get _____ things they knew. _____

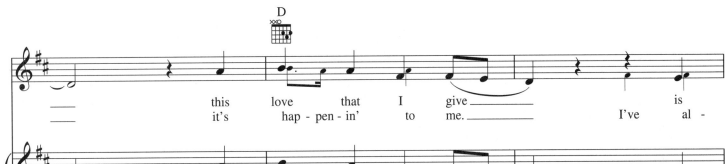

_____ _____
_____ _____
As sure as I live, _____
Well, it's eas - y to see _____

this love that I give _____ is
it's hap - pen - in' to me. _____ I've al -

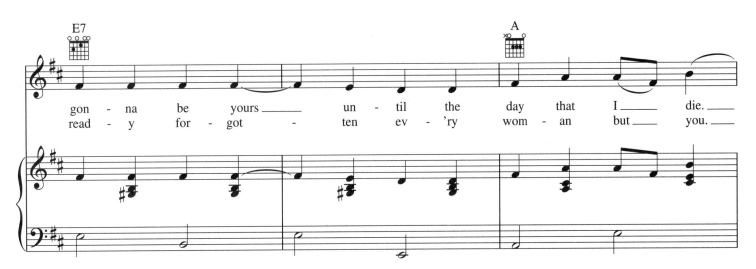

gon - na be yours _____ un - til the day that I _____ die. _____
read - y for - got - ten ev - 'ry wom - an but _____ you. _____

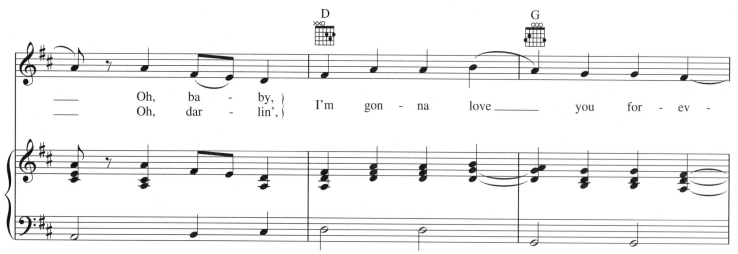

Oh, ba - by, } Oh, dar - lin', } I'm gon - na love _____ you for - ev -

- er, _____ _____ for - ev - er and ev -

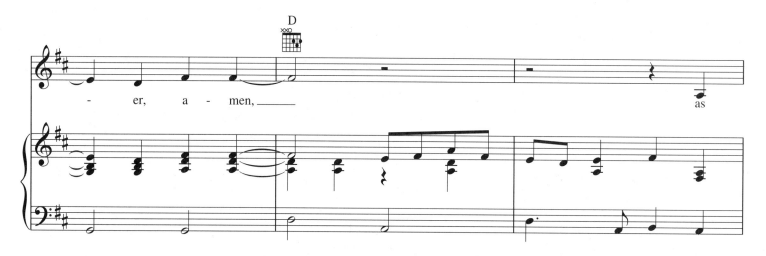

- er, a - men, _____ as

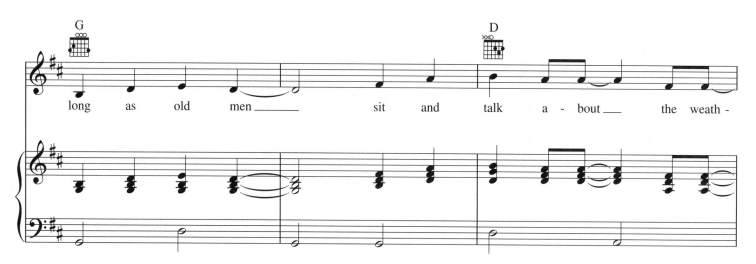

long as old men _____ sit and talk a - bout _____ the weath -

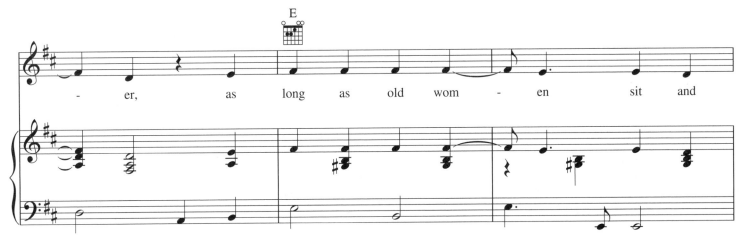

-er, as long as old wom-en sit and

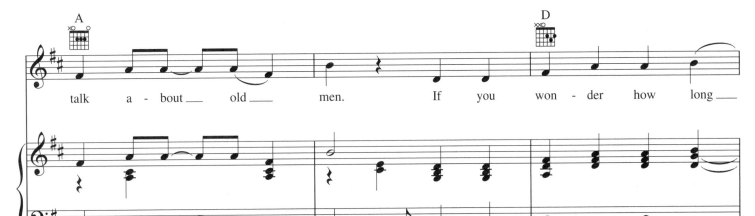

talk a-bout old men. If you won-der how long

I'll be faith-ful, I'll be
well, just

hap-py to tell you a-gain.
lis-ten to how this song ends.

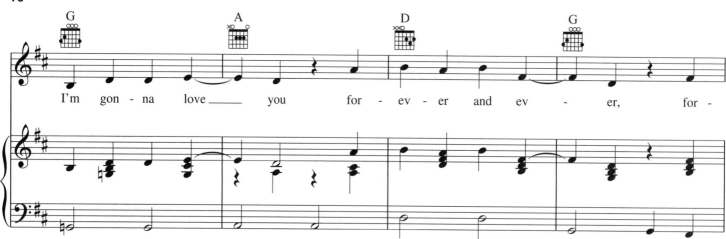

I'm gon-na love _____ you for - ev - er and ev - er, for -

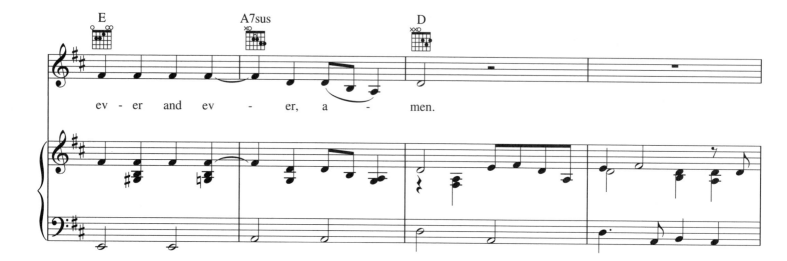

ev - er and ev - er, a - men.

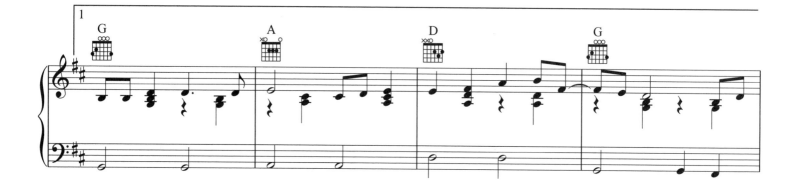

They say

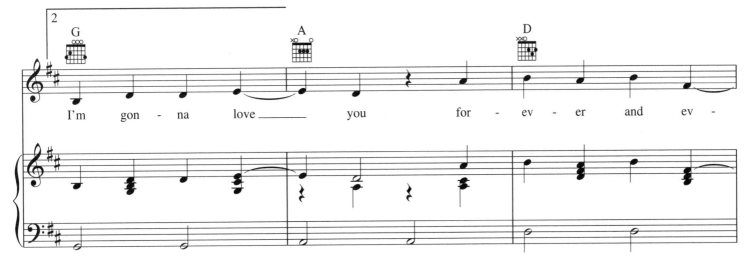

I'm gon-na love ____ you for - ev - er and ev -

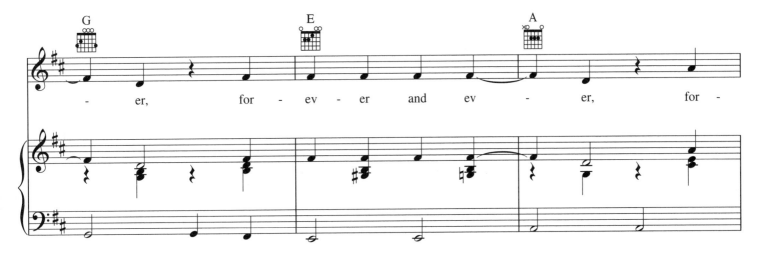

- er, for - ev - er and ev - er, for -

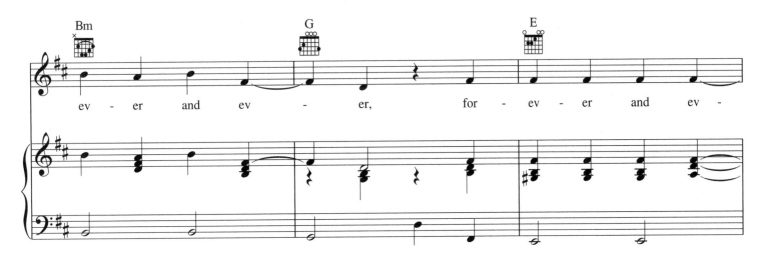

ev - er and ev - er, for - ev - er and ev -

- er, a - men. ____

FOUR WALLS

Words and Music by MARVIN J. MOORE
and GEORGE H. CAMPBELL, JR.

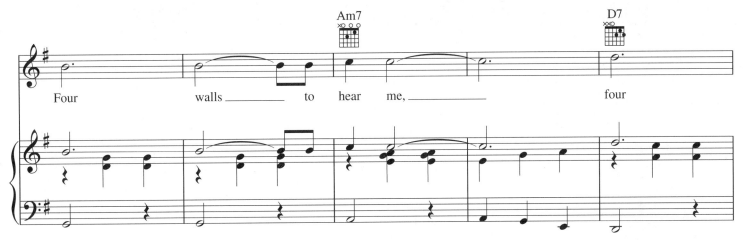

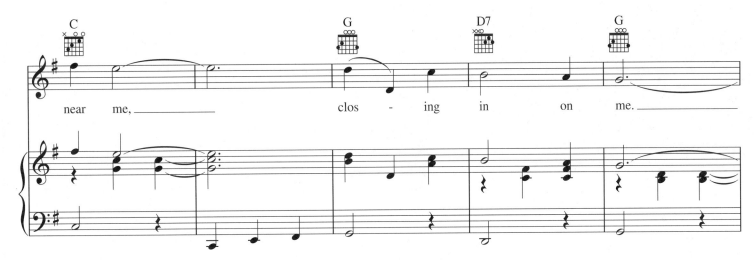

FUNNY HOW TIME SLIPS AWAY

Words and Music by
WILLIE NELSON

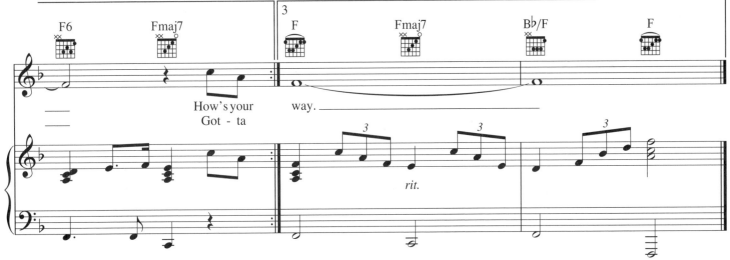

GOLDEN RING

Words and Music by BOBBY BRADDOCK
and RAFE VanHOY

it's just a cold me - tal - lic thing. On - ly love can make a

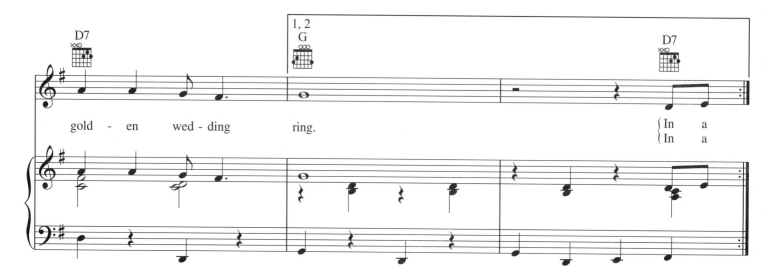

D7 **1, 2** **G** **D7**

gold - en wed - ding ring. {In a / In a

3 **G** **D.S. al Coda** **(lyric 1)** **D7**

ring. In a

CODA **G** **C**

rings there on dis -

rit.

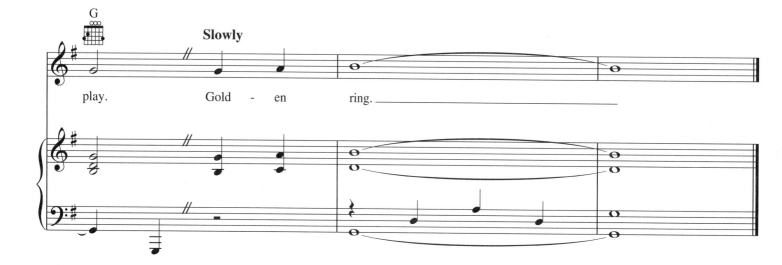

G **Slowly**

play. Gold - en ring.

I CAN'T STOP LOVING YOU

Words and Music by
DON GIBSON

Those hap-py hours _____ that we once

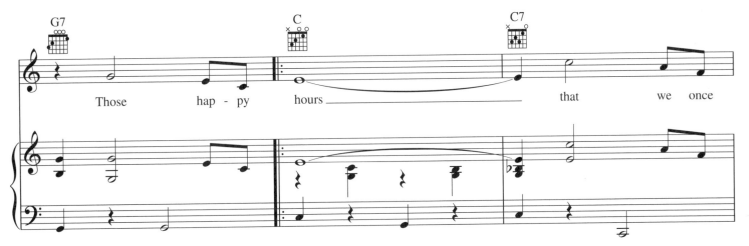

knew, _____ though long a - go, _____

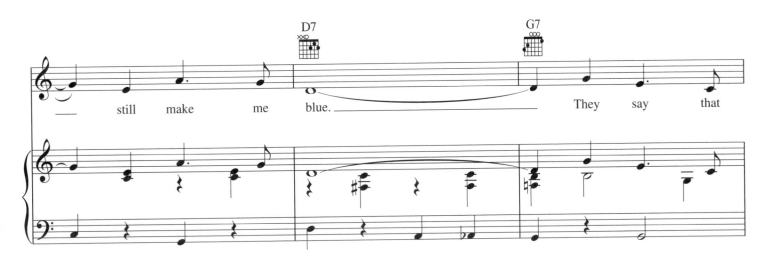

still make me blue. _____ They say that

time _____ heals _____ a bro-ken heart, _____

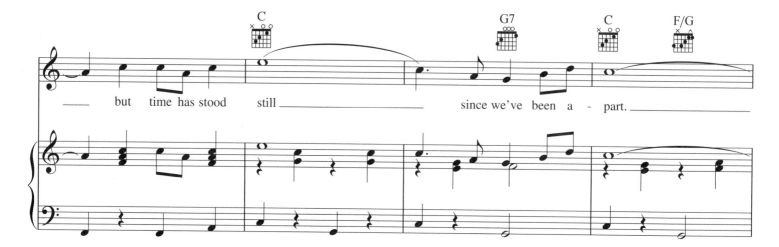

_____ but time has stood still _____ since we've been a - part. _____

I can't stop lov - ing you, _____ so I've made up my
I can't stop lov - ing you, _____ there's no use to

mind _____ to live in mem - o - ry _____
try. _____ Pre - tend there's some - one new; _____

HE STOPPED LOVING HER TODAY

Words and Music by BOBBY BRADDOCK
and CURLY PUTMAN

Very slowly

1. He said, "I'll love you 'til I die."   She told him, "You'll for-get in
2. wall;   went half cra-zy now and
3.-5. (See additional lyrics)

Am

time."   As the years went slow-ly by
then,   but he still loved her through it all,

G

she still preyed up-on his mind.
hop-ing she'd come back a-gain.

1-3
N.C.   D7

2. He kept her pic-ture on his
3. He kept some let-ters by his
4. I went to see him just to-

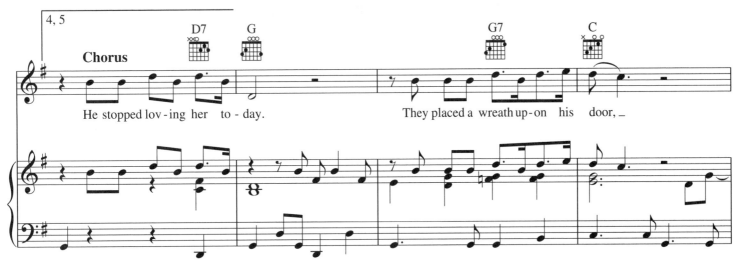

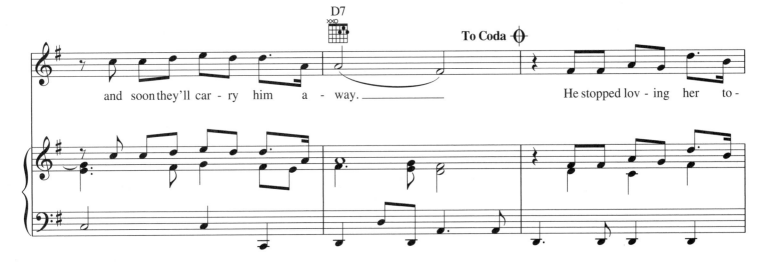

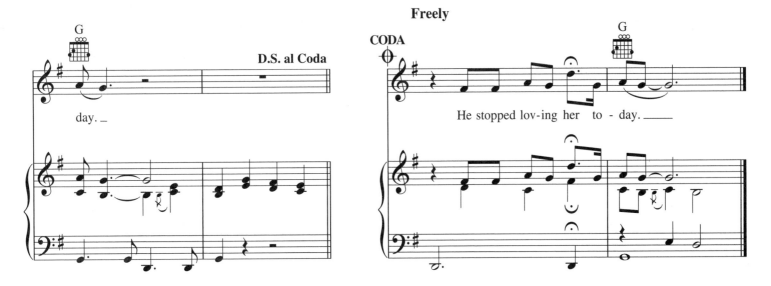

Additional Lyrics

3. He kept some letters by his bed, dated 1962.
   He had underlined in red every single, "I love you."

4. I went to see him just today, oh, but I didn't see no tears;
   All dressed up to go away, first time I'd seen him smile in years.
   Chorus

5. *(Spoken:) You know, she came to see him one last time.*
   We all wondered if she would.
   And it came running through my mind,
   This time he's over her for good.
   Chorus

HE'LL HAVE TO GO

Words and Music by JOE ALLISON
and AUDREY ALLISON

Moderately

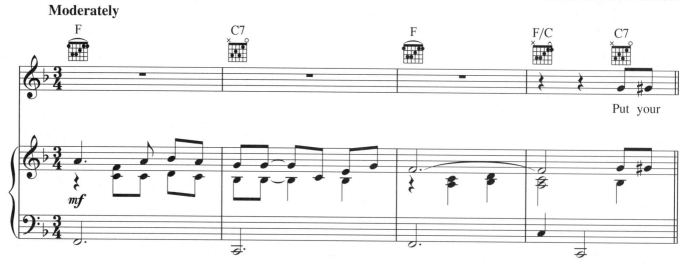

Put your

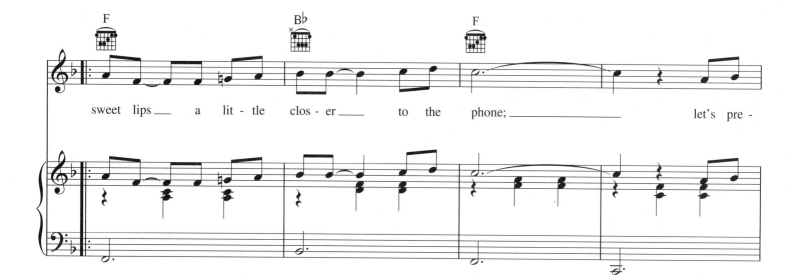

sweet lips a lit-tle clos-er to the phone; let's pre-

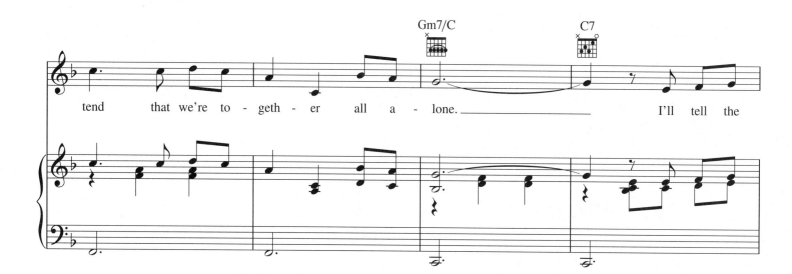

tend that we're to-geth-er all a-lone. I'll tell the

man   to turn the juke-box way down   low, _____   and you can

tell   your friend there   with   you __ he'll have to   go. _____   Whis-per

to me, ___ tell me, do   you love me   true, _____   or is

he hold-ing   you   the way I   do? _____   Though love is

blind, make up your mind; I've got to know. _____ Should I

hang up ___ or will you tell him ___ he'll have to go? _____ You can't

say the words I want to hear while you're with an - oth - er man. If you

want me, an - swer "Yes" or "No"; dar - ling, I will un - der - stand. Put your

I BELIEVE IN YOU

Words and Music by ROGER COOK
and SAM HOGIN

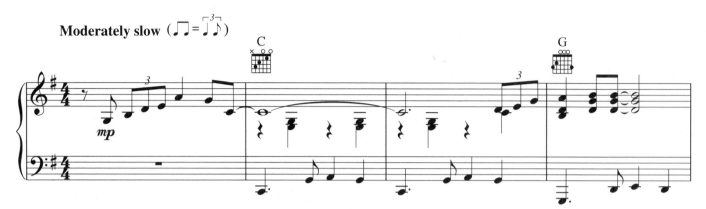

I don't be-lieve in su-per-stars,__ or-gan-ic food__ and for-eign cars.__ I
don't be-lieve that heav-en waits__ for on-ly those__ who con-gre-gate.__ I

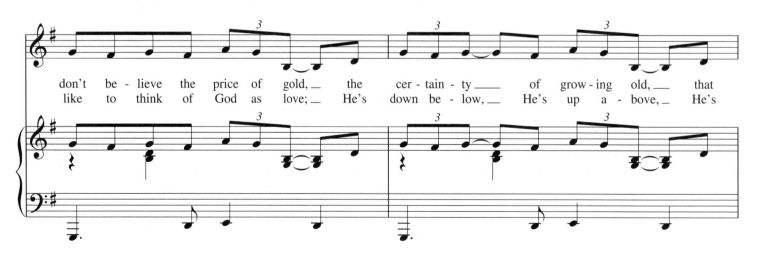

don't be-lieve the price of gold,__ the cer-tain-ty__ of grow-ing old,__ that
like to think of God as love;__ He's down be-low,__ He's up a-bove,__ He's

I know with all my cer-tain-ty ___ what's go-in' on with you and me ___ is a good thing.

It's true — I be-lieve in you.

I don't be-lieve vir-gin-i-ty ___ is as com-mon as ___ it used to be, ___ in

work-in' days and sleep-in' nights, ___ that black is black ___ and white is white, ___ that Su-per-man and Rob-in Hood ___ are

I FALL TO PIECES

Words and Music by HANK COCHRAN
and HARLAN HOWARD

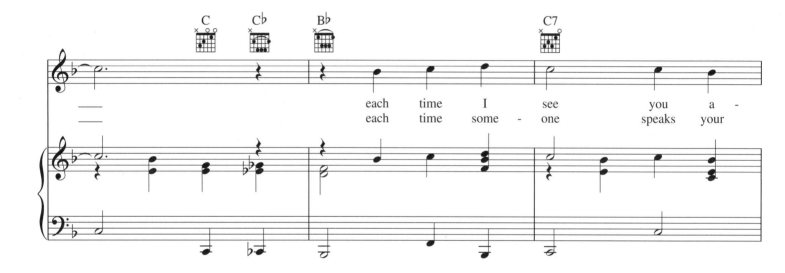

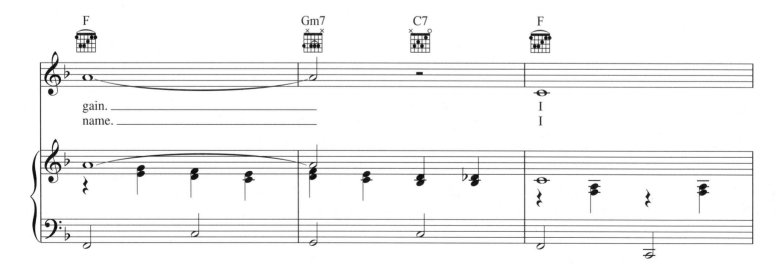

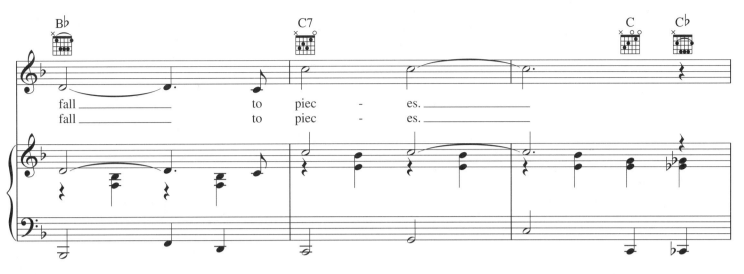

fall _____ to piec - es. _____
fall _____ to piec - es. _____

How can I be just your friend? _____
Time on - ly adds to the flame. _____

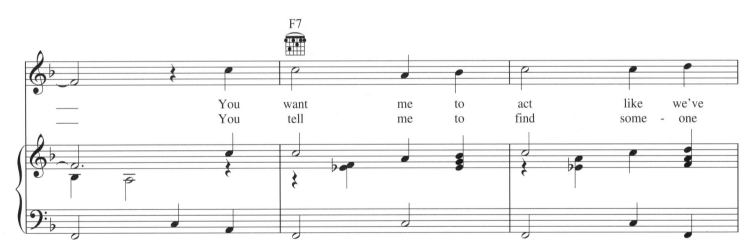

___ You want me to act like we've
___ You tell me to find some - one

nev - er kissed. _____ You want me to for - me
else to love, _____ some - one who'll love me

get,   pre - tend we've nev - er met. _____ And I've
too   the way you used to do. _____ But each

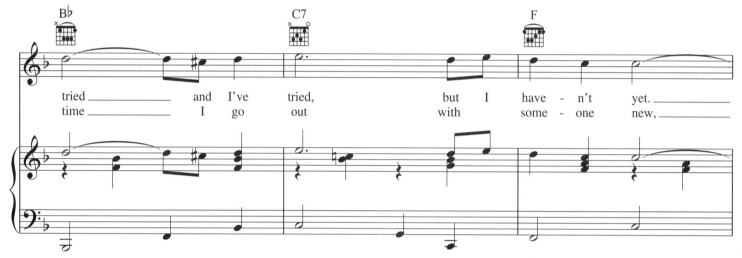

tried _____ and I've tried,   but I have - n't yet. _____
time _____ I go out with some - one new, _____

___ You walk by   and I fall to
___ you walk by   and I fall to

piec - es. _____

piec - es. _____

rall.

I STILL MISS SOMEONE

Words and Music by JOHNNY R. CASH
and ROY CASH, JR.

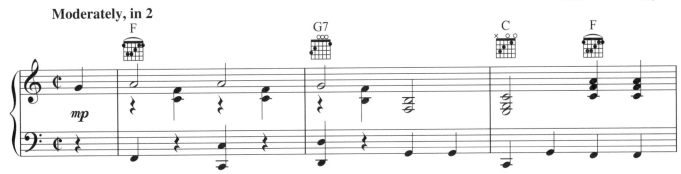

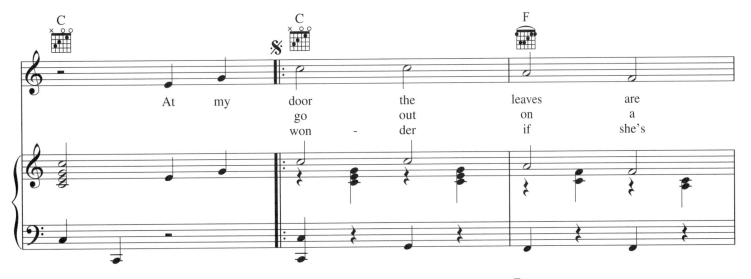

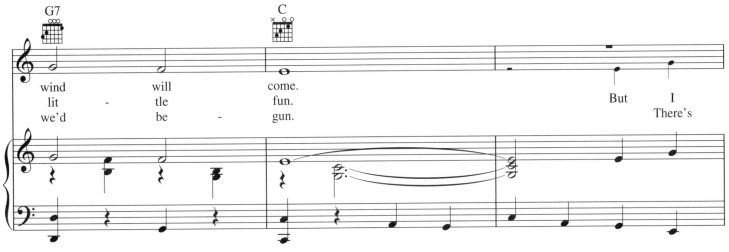

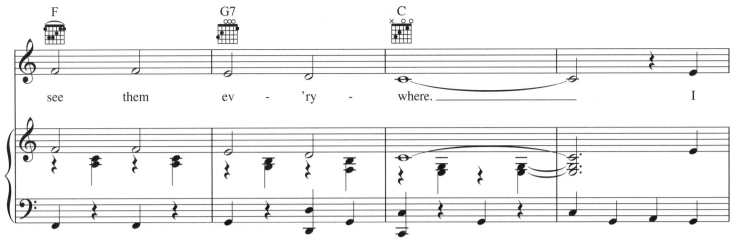

see them ev - 'ry - where. _____ I

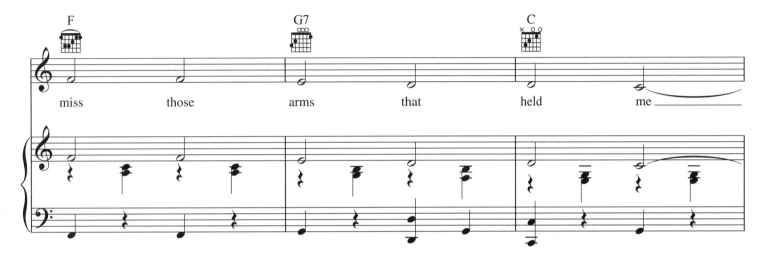

miss those arms that held me _____

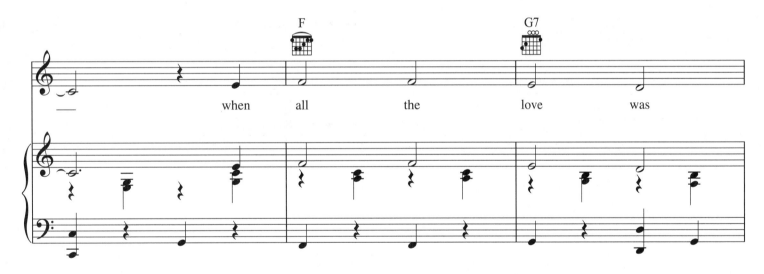

when all the love was

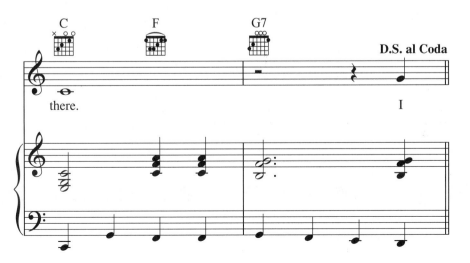

there. I

D.S. al Coda

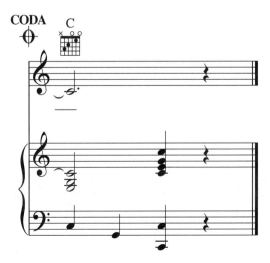

CODA

I LOVE

Words and Music by
TOM T. HALL

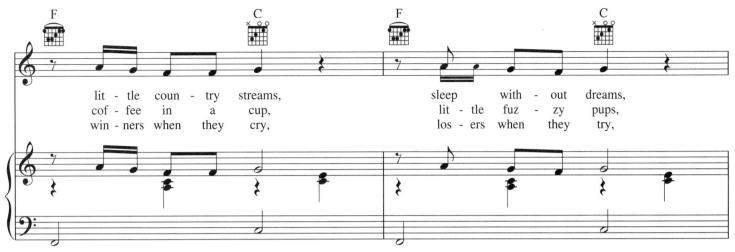

lit - tle coun - try streams,
cof - fee in a cup,
win - ners when they cry,

sleep with - out dreams,
lit - tle fuz - zy pups,
los - ers when they try,

Sun - day School in May ___ and hay.
bour - bon in a glass ___ and grass.
mu - sic when it's good ___ and life.

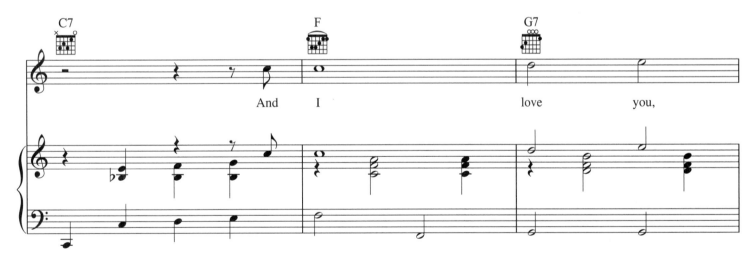

And I love you,

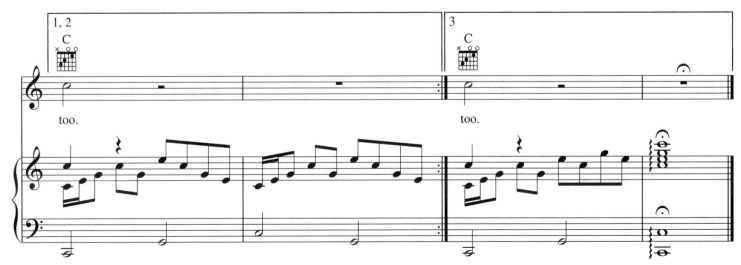

too.

too.

I LOVE YOU

from the Paramount Motion Picture RUNAWAY BRIDE

Words and Music by TAMMY HYLER,
KEITH FOLLESE and ADRIENNE FOLLESE

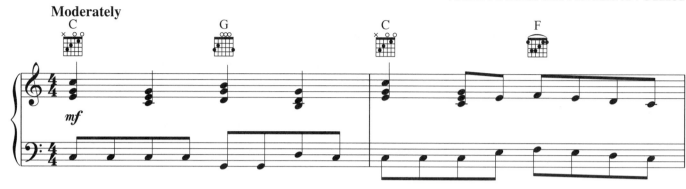

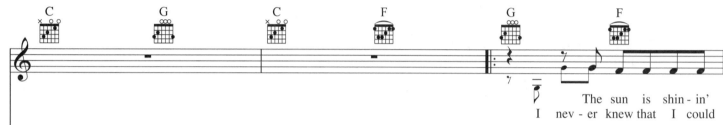

The sun is shin-in'
I nev-er knew that I could

ev-'ry day, clouds nev-er get in the way for you and me.___
feel like this, can hard-ly wait till our next kiss. You're so cool.___

I've known you just a
If I'm dream-in', please don't

week or two, but, ba - by, I'm so in - to you can hard - ly breathe. __
wake me up 'cause, ba - by, I can't get e - nough of what you ___ do. ___

___ And I'm in, _____ so to - tal - ly wrapped __
___ And I'm in, _____ so e - lec - tri - c'ly charged __

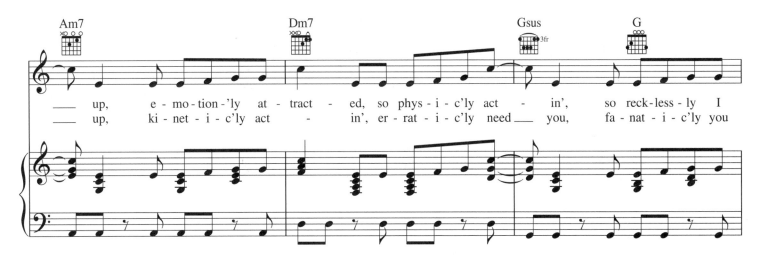

___ up, e - mo - tion - 'ly at - tract - ed, so phys - i - c'ly act - in', so reck - less - ly I
___ up, ki - net - i - c'ly act - in', er - rat - i - c'ly need ___ you, fa - nat - i - c'ly you

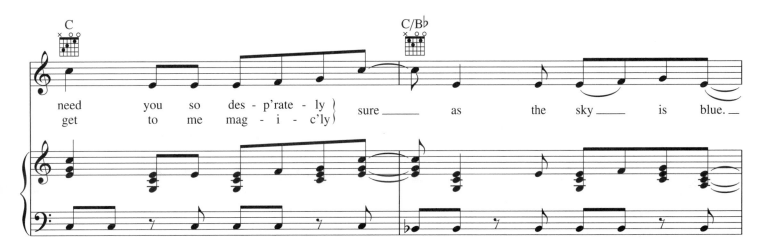

need you so des - p'rate - ly ⎫
get to me mag - i - c'ly ⎭ sure ___ as the sky ___ is blue. __

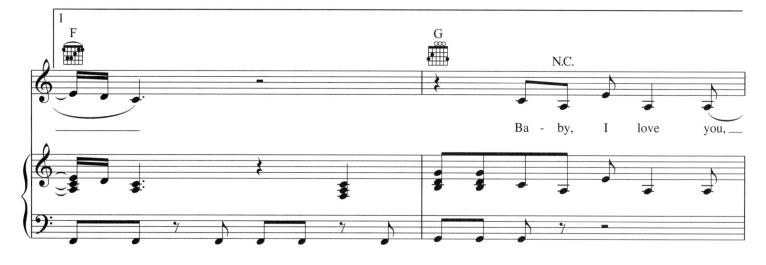

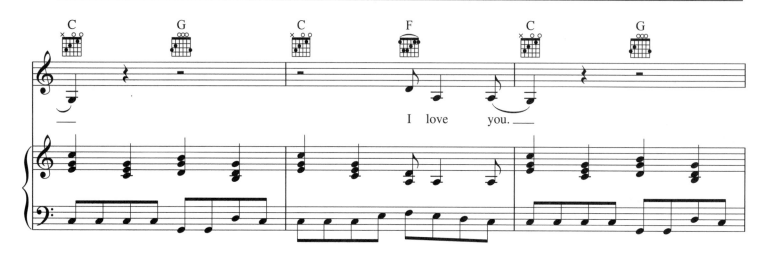

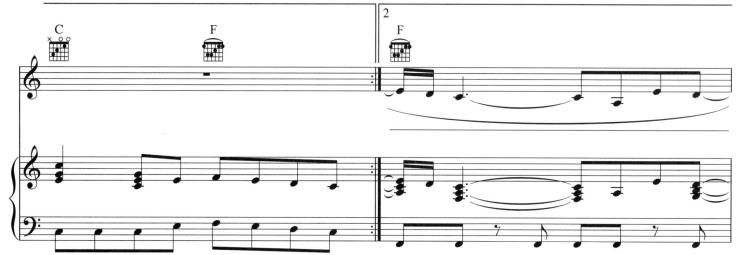

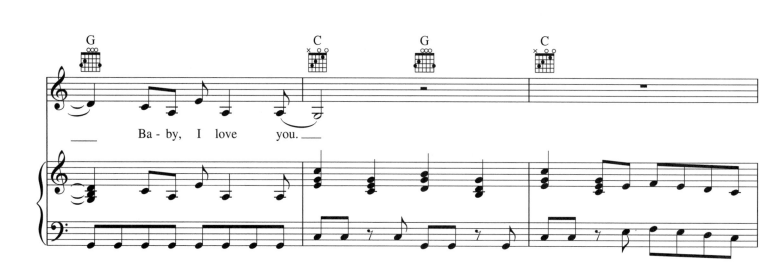

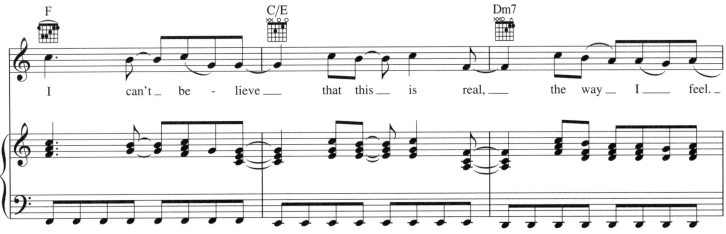

I can't be-lieve that this is real, the way I feel.

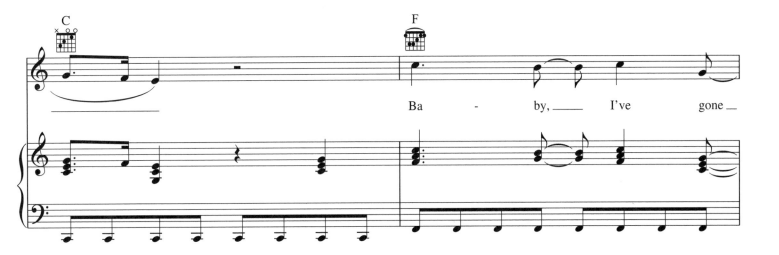

Ba - by, I've gone

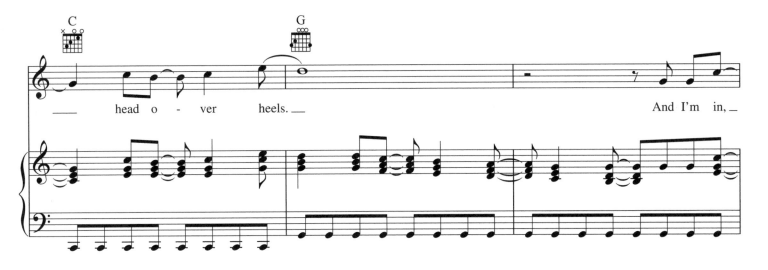

head o - ver heels. And I'm in,

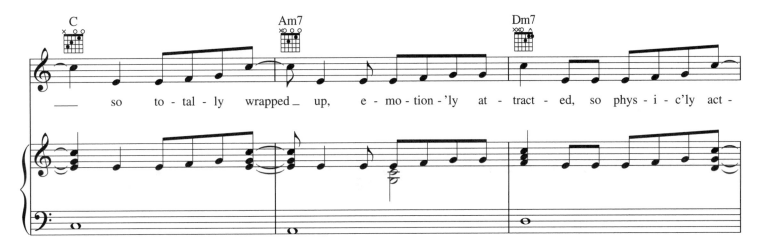

so to-tal-ly wrapped up, e-mo-tion-'ly at-tract-ed, so phys-i-c'ly act-

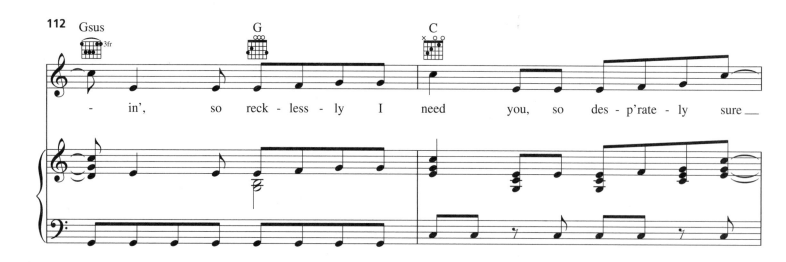

-in', so reck-less-ly I need you, so des-p'rate-ly sure ___

___ as the sky ___ is blue, ___ yeah. ___

And I'm in, ___ so e-lec-tri-c'ly charged _

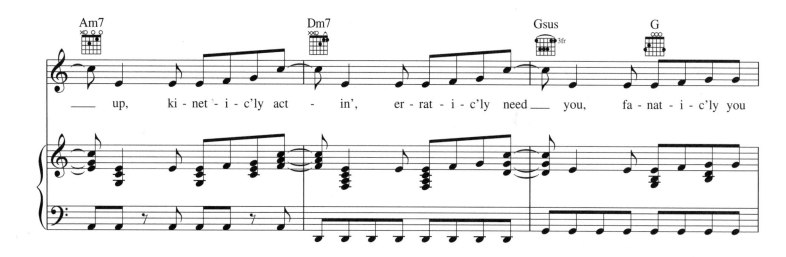

___ up, ki-net-i-c'ly act-in', er-rat-i-c'ly need ___ you, fa-nat-i-c'ly you

get to me mag - i - c'ly sure _____ as the sky _____ is blue. _____

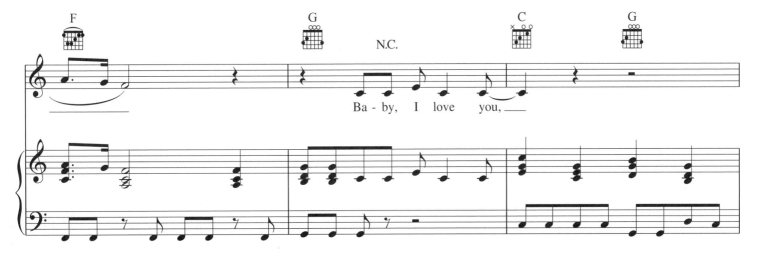

Ba - by, I love you, _____

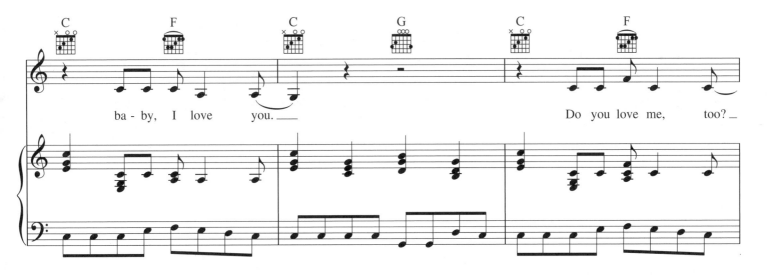

ba - by, I love you. _____ Do you love me, too? _____

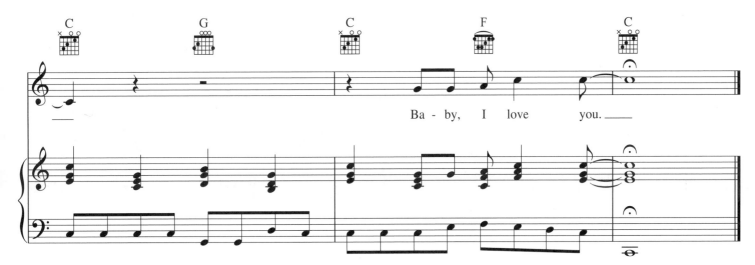

Ba - by, I love you. _____

I WALK THE LINE

Words and Music by
JOHN R. CASH

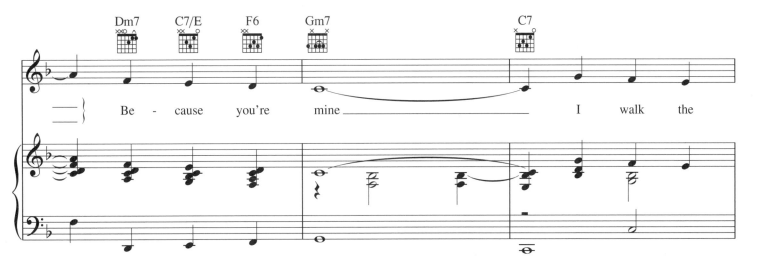

Additional Lyrics

3. As sure as night is dark and day is light,
   I keep you on my mind both day and night.
   And happiness I've known proves that it's right.
   Because you're mine I walk the line.

4. You've got a way to keep me on your side.
   You give me cause for love that I can't hide.
   For you I know I'd even try to turn the tide.
   Because you're mine I walk the line.

5. I keep a close watch on this heart of mine.
   I keep my eyes wide open all the time.
   I keep the ends out for the tie that binds.
   Because you're mine I walk the line.

I WILL ALWAYS LOVE YOU

Words and Music by
DOLLY PARTON

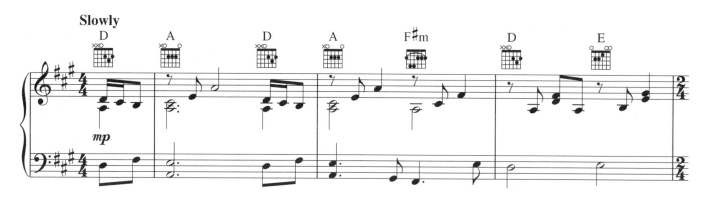

of you each step___ of the way._____ And
know that I'm not___ what you need._____ But   } I_____ will
all of this, I   wish you love.   *(Sung:)* And

al - ways_ love_ you._____ I___ will al - ways_ love_

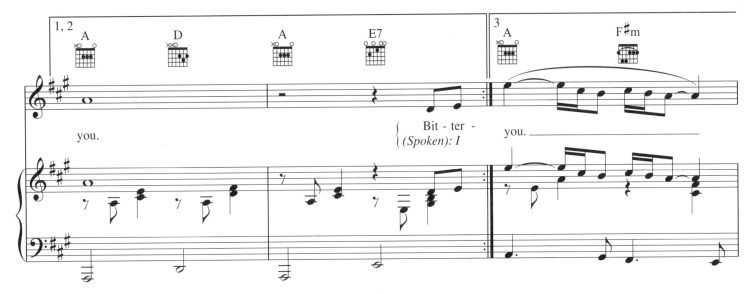

1, 2

you.

Bit - ter -
(Spoken): I   you._____

3

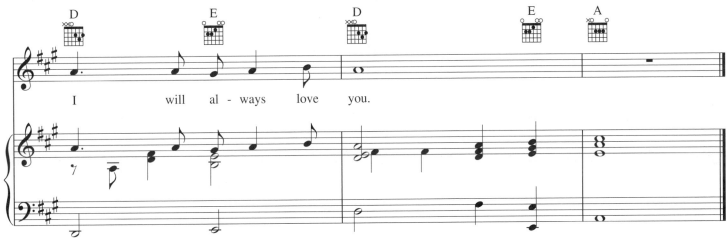

I   will al - ways love you.

I'LL GO ON LOVING YOU

Words and Music by
KIERAN KANE

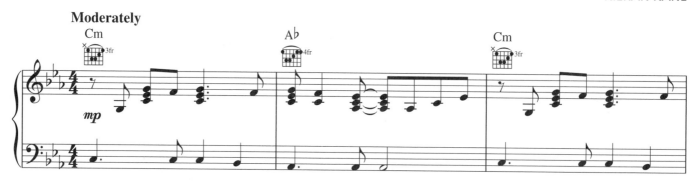

Spoken: (1., D.S.) *When I look into your soft green eyes,*
(2.) *Be it the wind or the rain,*

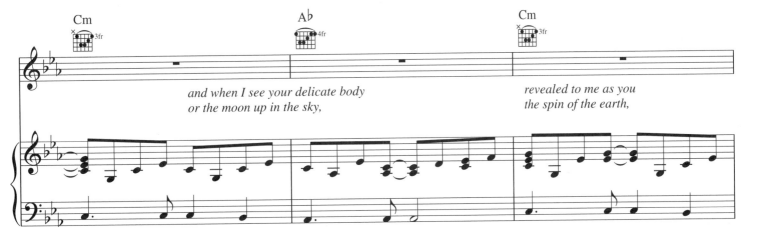

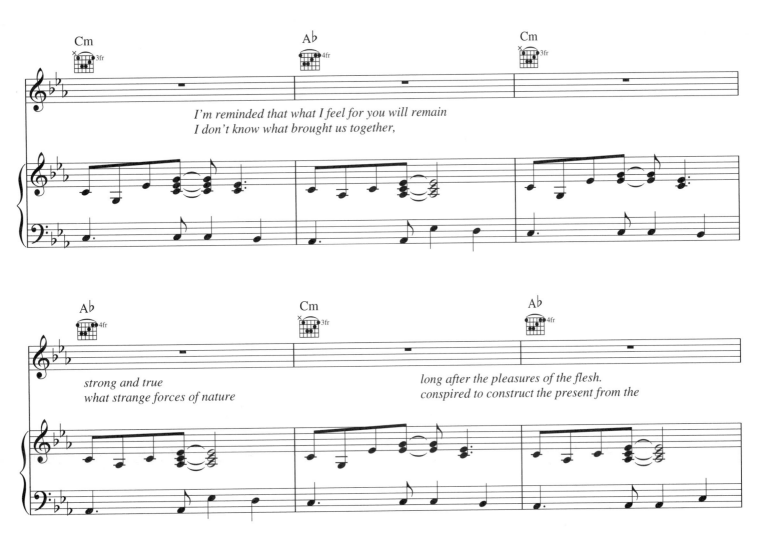

past.

And⎫
But ⎭ I'll go on ____

lov - ing you, ____ I'll go on ____ lov - ing ____ you, ____

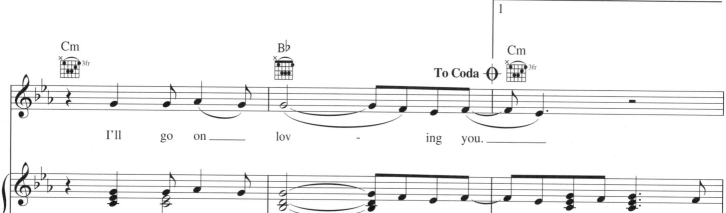

I'll go on ____ lov - ing you. ____

To Coda

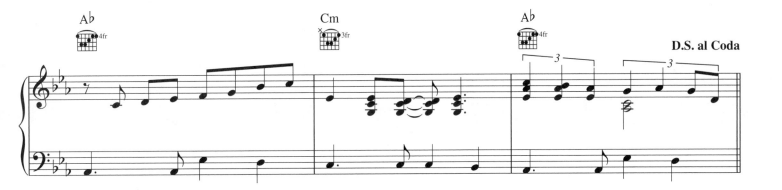

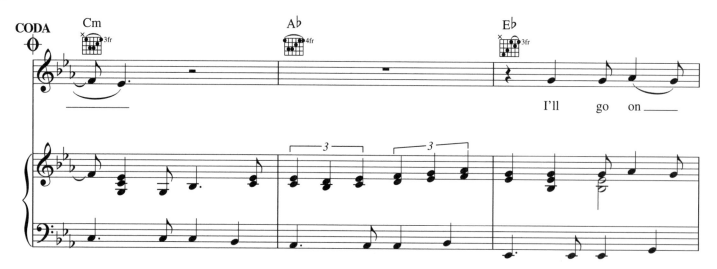

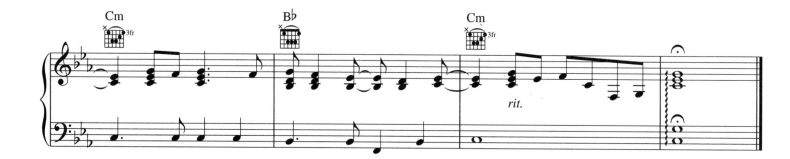

IF I COULD ONLY WIN YOUR LOVE

Words and Music by CHARLIE LOUVIN
and IRA LOUVIN

love, I'd give my all ___ to make it live; you'll nev-er know ___ how

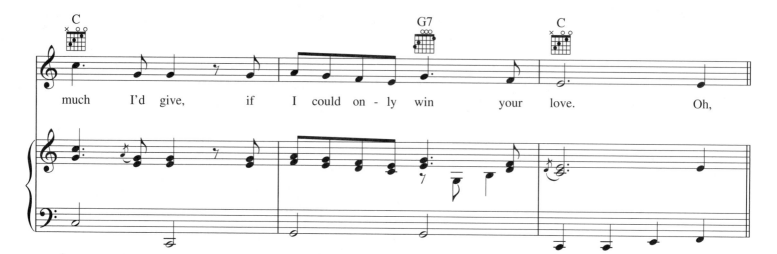

much I'd give, if I could on-ly win your love. Oh,

how can I ev-er say how I crave your love when you're

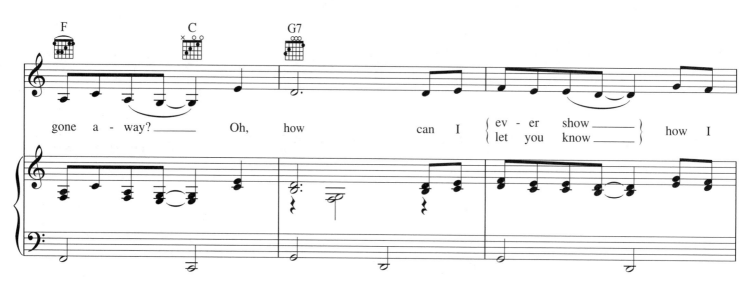

gone a-way? ___ Oh, how can I { ev-er show ___ } how I
{ let you know ___ }

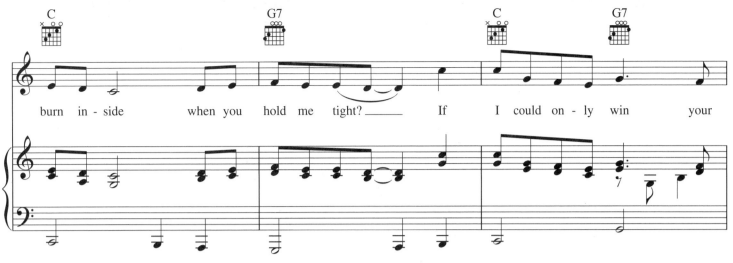

burn in - side   when you hold me tight? _____   If   I   could on - ly win   your

love,   I'd give my all _____ to make   it live;

you'll nev - er know ___ how much I'd give,   if   I   could on - ly win   your

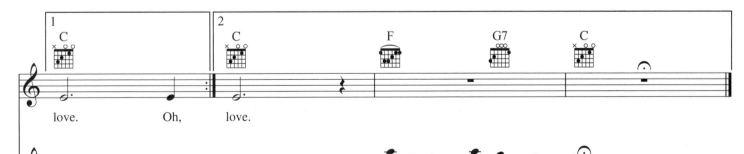

love.   Oh,   love.

I'M SO LONESOME I COULD CRY

Words and Music by
HANK WILLIAMS

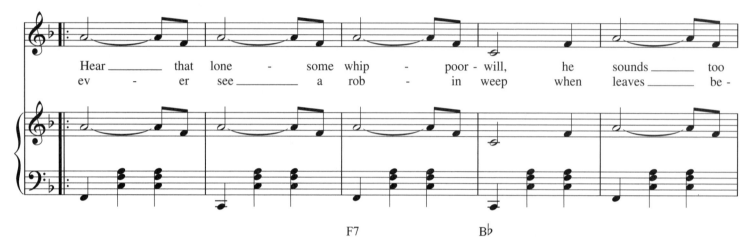

Hear _____ that lone - some whip - poor - will, he sounds _____ too
ev - er see _____ a rob - in weep when leaves _____ be -

blue _____ to fly. _____ The mid - night train is
gan _____ to die. _____ That means he's lost the

whin - ing low. I'm so lone - some I could _ cry. _____
will to live. I'm so lone - some I could _ cry. _____

I've nev - er seen _____ a night _____ so long, when
The si - lence of _____ a fall - ing star when lights

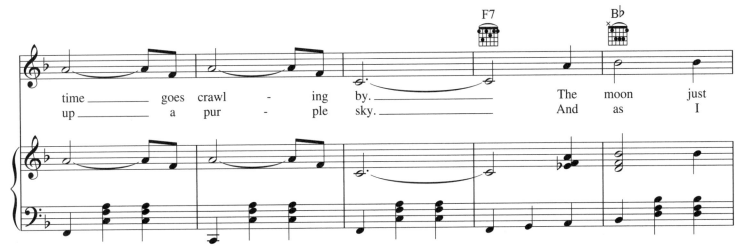

time _____ goes crawl - ing by. _____ The moon just
up _____ a pur - ple sky. _____ And as I

went be - hind a cloud to ___ hide its face and ___
won - der where you are I'm so lone - some I could ___

cry. _____ Did you cry. _____

IF LOVING YOU IS WRONG
I DON'T WANT TO BE RIGHT

Words and Music by HOMER BANKS,
CARL HAMPTON and RAYMOND JACKSON

Moderately

If lov - in' you is wrong, I don't want to be right. If
Am I wrong to fall so deep-ly in love with you,

be - ing right _ means be - ing with-out _ you, I'd rath - er live a wrong-do-ing life. Your
know-ing I got a wife and two lit-tle chil-dren de - pend - ing on me, too? But

Copyright © 1971 IRVING MUSIC, INC.
Copyright Renewed
All Rights Reserved Used by Permission

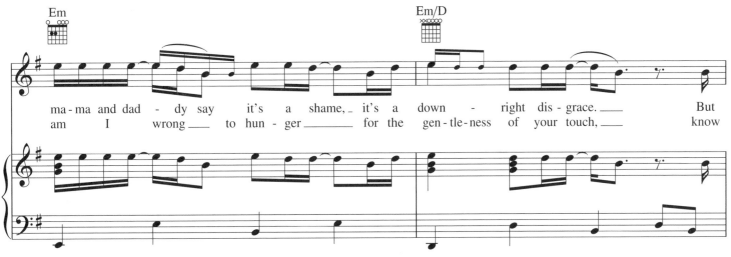

ma-ma and dad-dy say it's a shame,_ it's a down-right dis-grace.___ But

am I wrong_ to hun-ger___ for the gen-tle-ness of your touch,_ know

long as I got you by my side_ I don't care what your peo-ple say._____ Your

ing I got some-one else at home_____ who needs me just as much._____ And

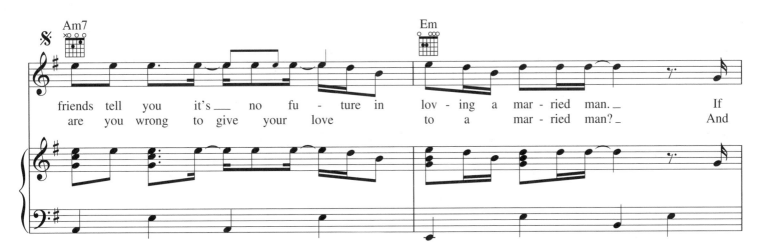

friends tell you it's_ no fu-ture in lov-ing a mar-ried man._ If

are you wrong to give your love to a mar-ried man?_ And

I can't see you when I want_ to I'll see you when_ I can._____ If

am I wrong for try-ing to hold on to the best thing I ev-er had?_ If

IF TOMORROW NEVER COMES

Words and Music by KENT BLAZY
and GARTH BROOKS

Slowly

1. Some - times late at night, ___
2. *(See additional lyrics)*

With pedal

I lie a - wake ___ and watch ___ her sleep - ing. ___

She's lost in peace - ful dreams, ___ so I turn

off the lights ___ and lay there in the dark. ___

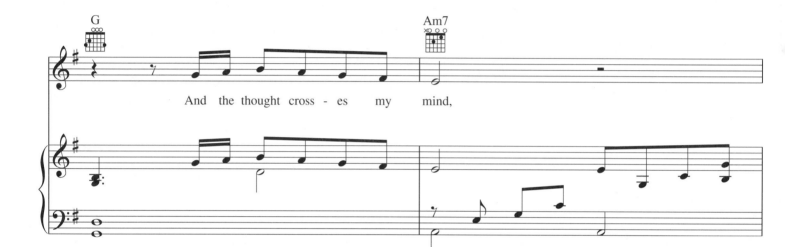

And the thought cross - es my mind,

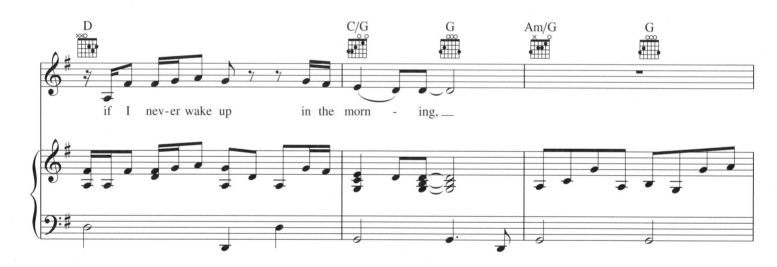

if I nev-er wake up in the morn - ing, ___

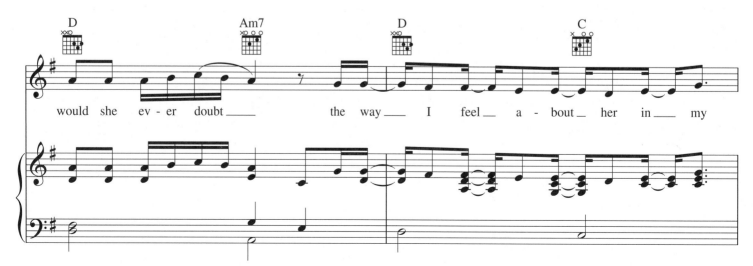

would she ev - er doubt ___ the way ___ I feel ___ a - bout ___ her in ___ my

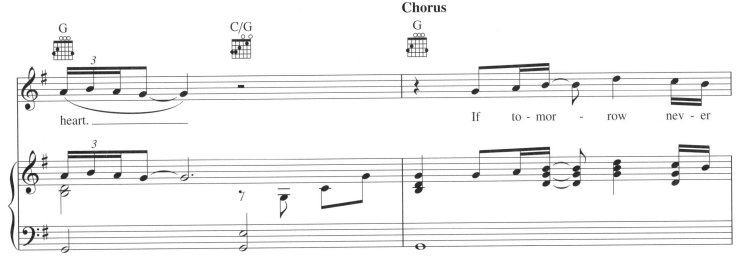

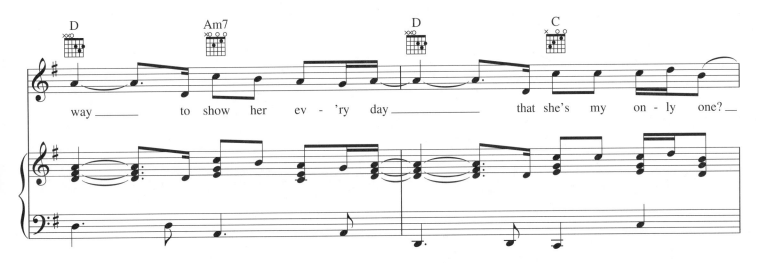

Chorus

heart. _____ If to - mor - row nev - er

comes, _____ will she know how much I

loved her? _____ Did I try in ev - 'ry

way _____ to show her ev - 'ry day _____ that she's my on - ly one? __

And if my time on earth were

through, and she must face this world with-

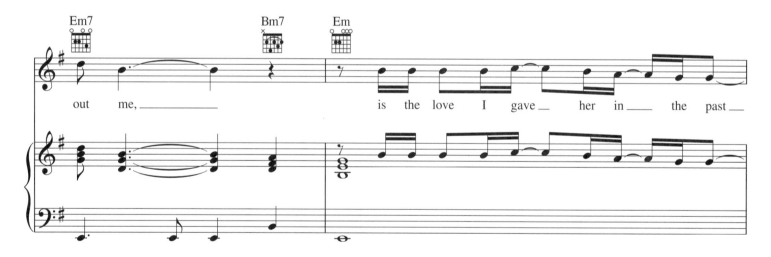

out me, is the love I gave her in the past

gon-na be e-nough to last if to-mor-row nev-er

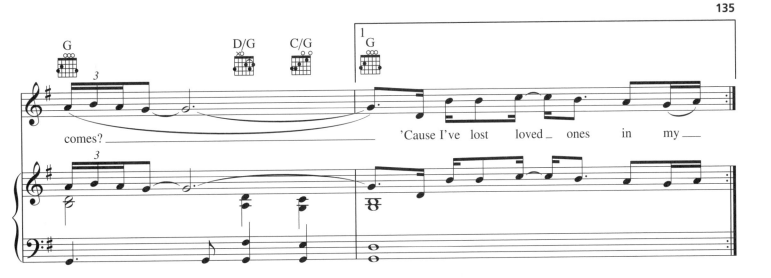

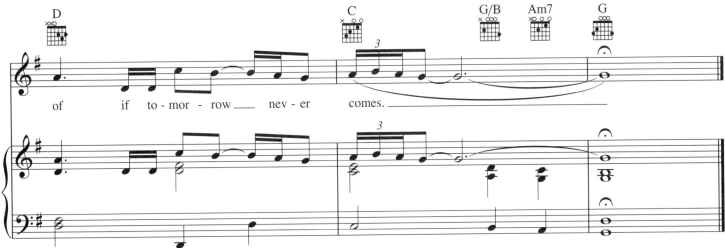

Additional Lyrics

2. 'Cause I've lost loved ones in my life
Who never knew how much I loved them.
Now I live with the regret
That my true feelings for them never were revealed.
So I made a promise to myself
To say each day how much she means to me
And avoid that circumstance
Where there's no second chance to tell her how I feel. ('Cause)
Chorus

IT WAS ALMOST LIKE A SONG

Lyric by HAL DAVID
Music by ARCHIE JORDAN

Relaxed

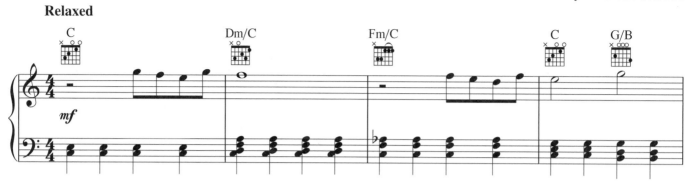

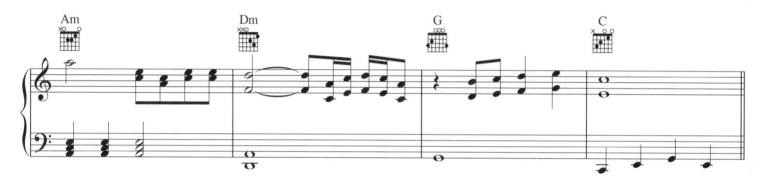

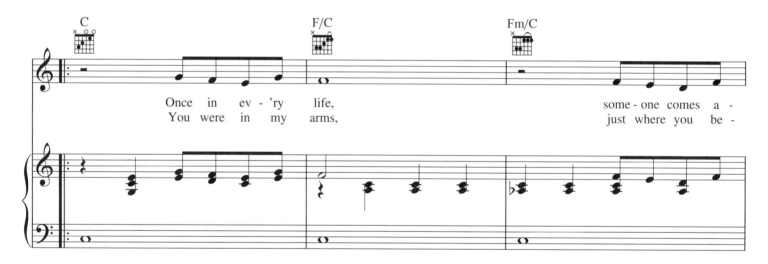

Once in ev-'ry life,   some - one comes a -
You were in my arms,   just where you be -

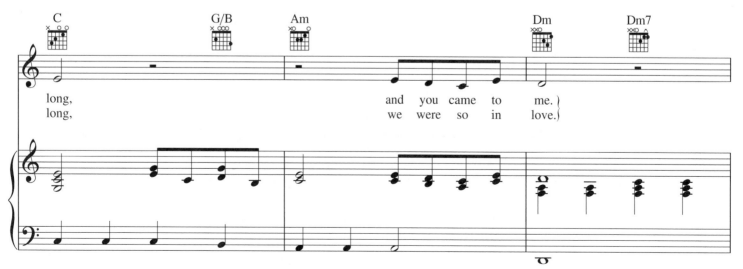

long,   and you came to me.)
long,   we were so in love.)

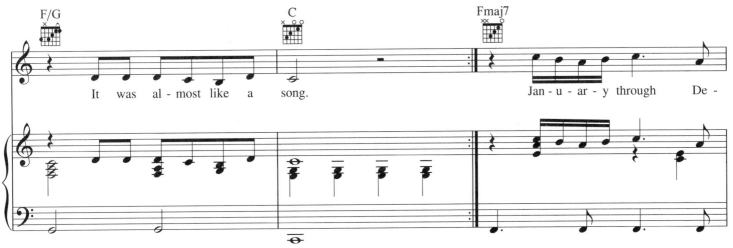

It was al-most like a song. Jan-u-ar-y through De-

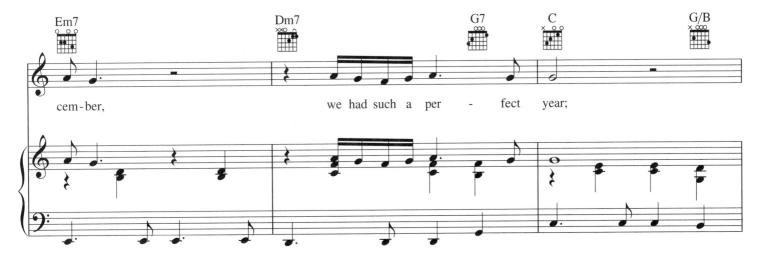

cem-ber, we had such a per - fect year;

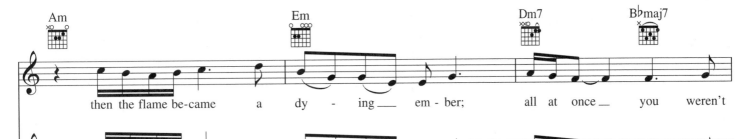

then the flame be-came a dy - ing em-ber; all at once you weren't

there. Now my bro-ken heart

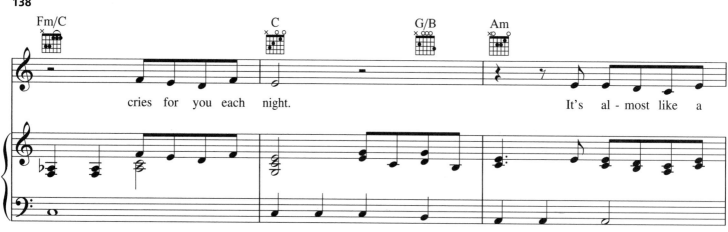

cries for you each night. It's al-most like a

song, — but it's too sad to write.

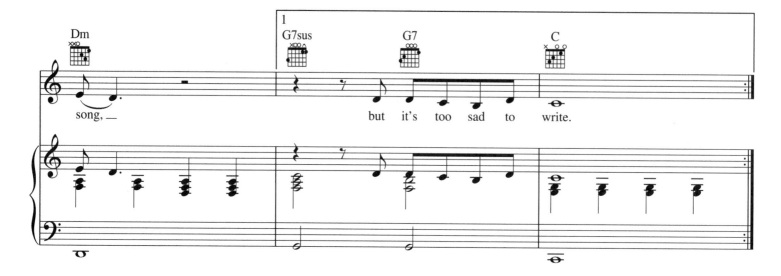

but it's too sad to write. ____

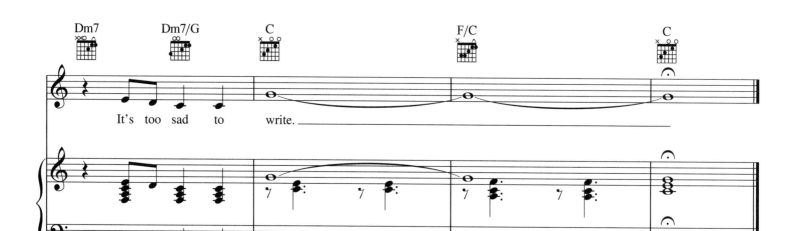

It's too sad to write. ____

KISS AN ANGEL GOOD MORNIN'

Words and Music by
BEN PETERS

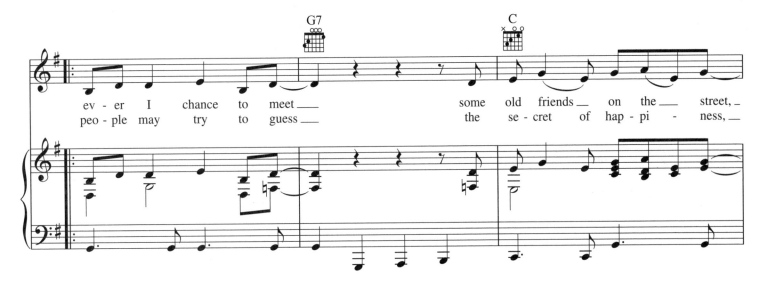

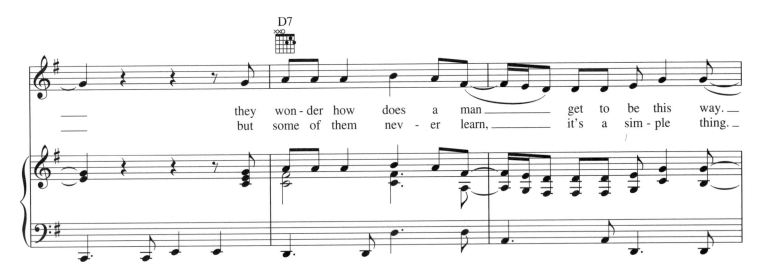

IT'S FOUR IN THE MORNING

Words and Music by
JERRY CHESNUT

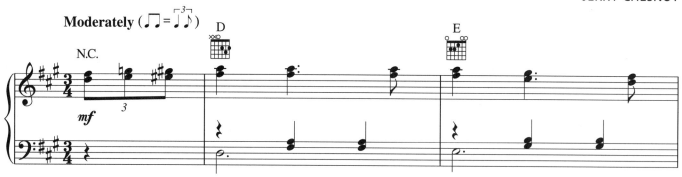

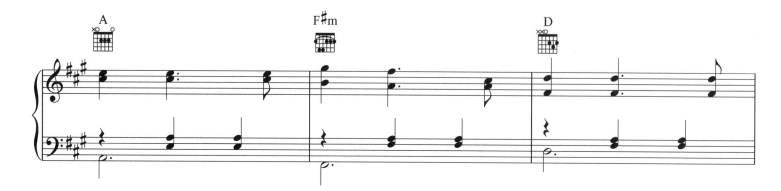

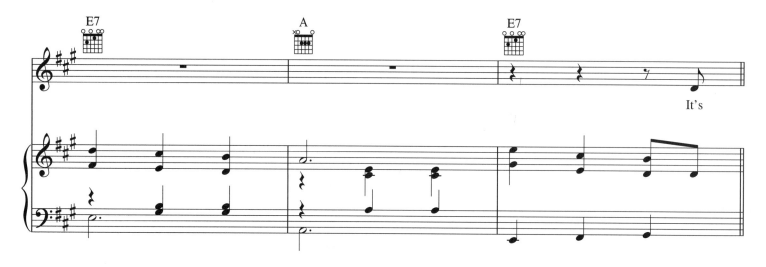

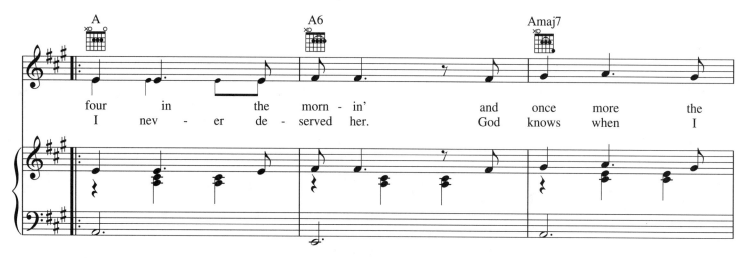

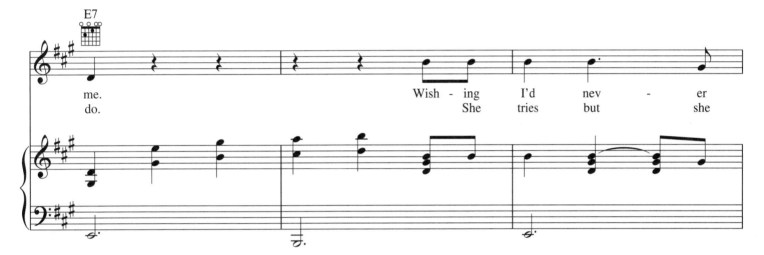

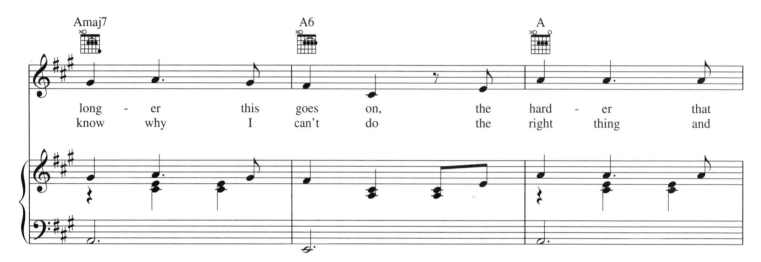

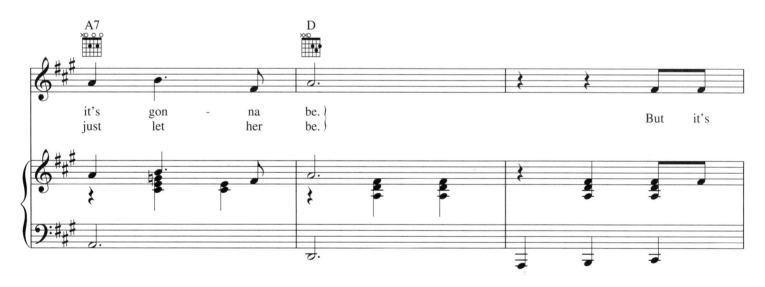

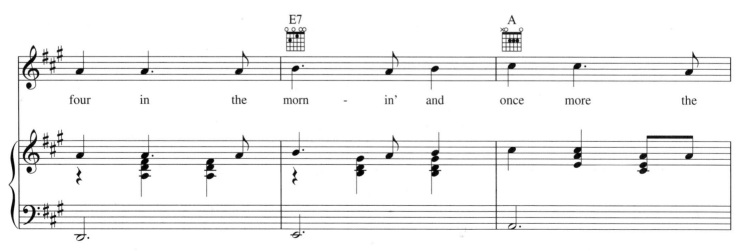

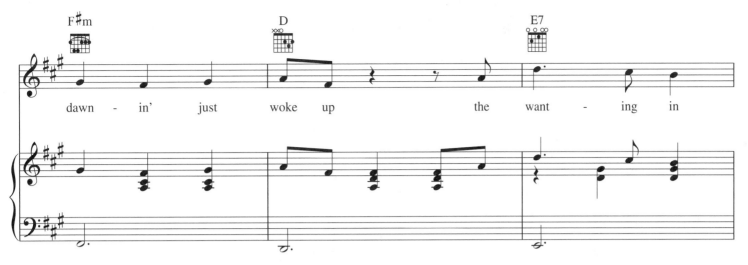

dawn - in' just woke up   the   want - ing in

me.

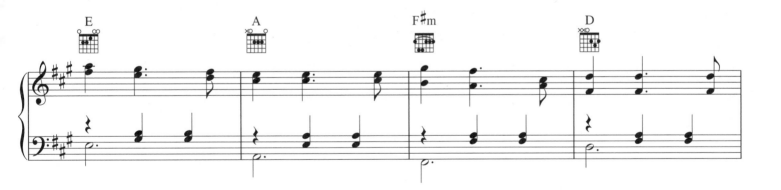

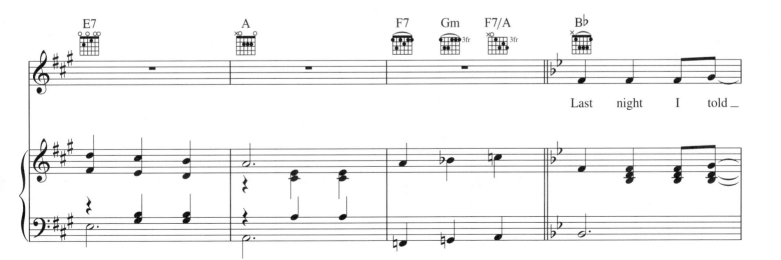

Last night I told __

_____ her this time _____ it's all o - ver, mak - in' ten times _____ I've

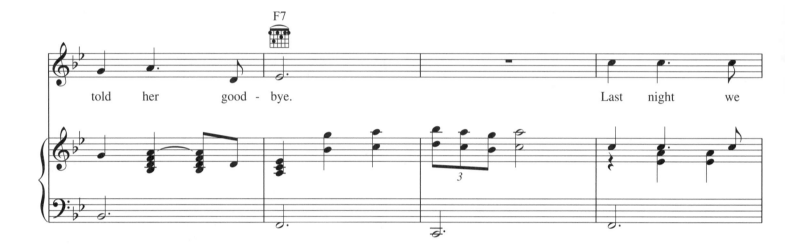

told her good - bye. Last night we

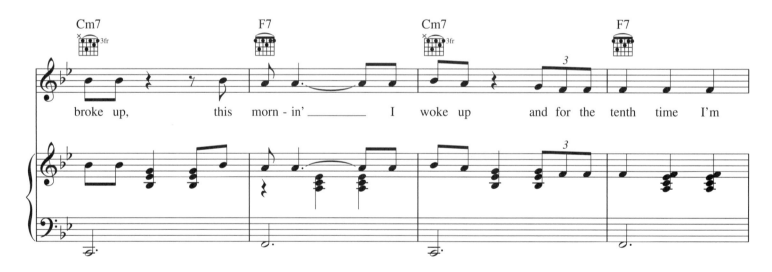

broke up, this morn - in' _____ I woke up and for the tenth time I'm

chang - in' my mind. I saw more love _____

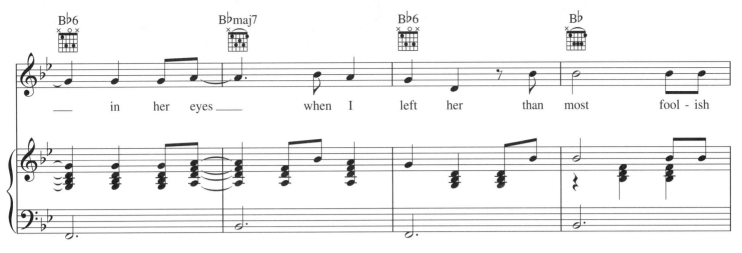

in her eyes _____ when I left her than most fool - ish

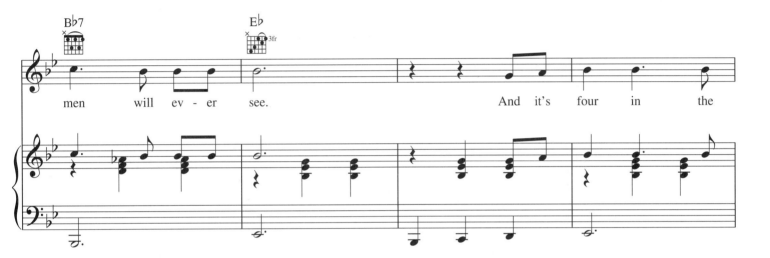

men will ev - er see. And it's four in the

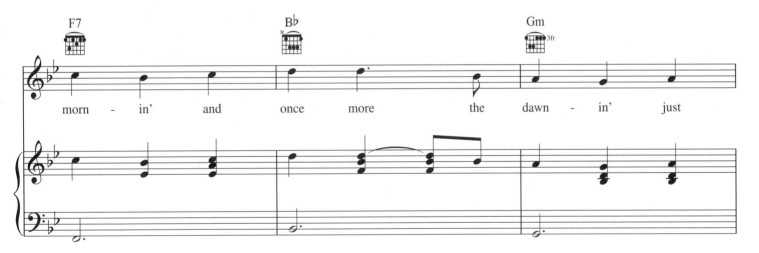

morn - in' and once more the dawn - in' just

woke up the want - ing in me.

JUST SOMEONE I USED TO KNOW

Words and Music by
JACK CLEMENT

Moderately slow

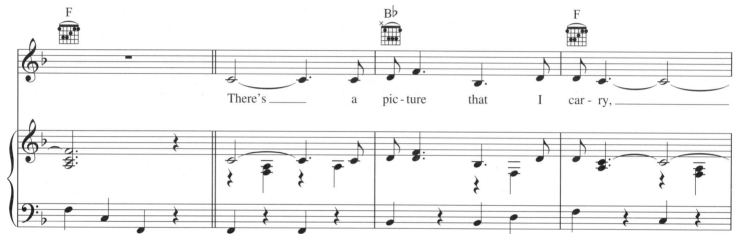

There's ___ a pic-ture that I car-ry, ___

___ one we made ___ some time a - go. ___

When they ask who's in the pic-ture with me, ___

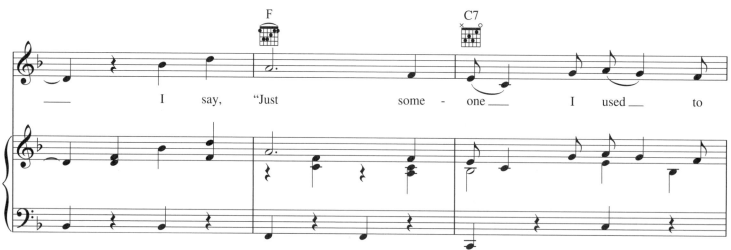

I say, "Just some - one ___ I used ___ to

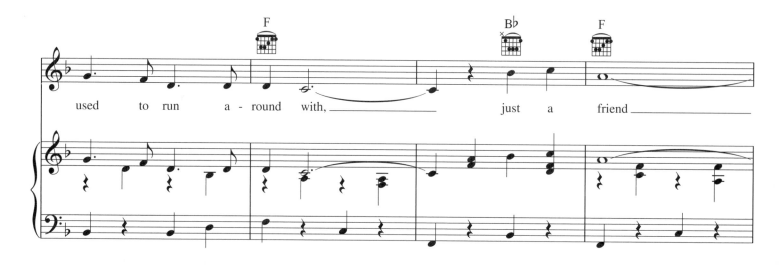

know. _____ Just some - one _____ I

used to run a - round with, _____ just a friend _____

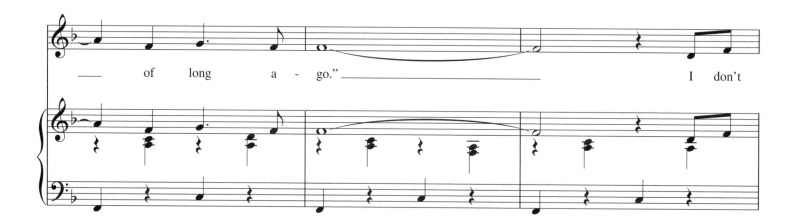

___ of long a - go." _____ I don't

tell them how lost I am with - out you, _____

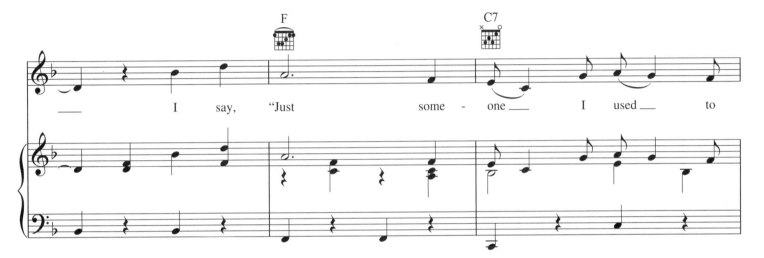

_____ I say, "Just some - one ___ I used ___ to

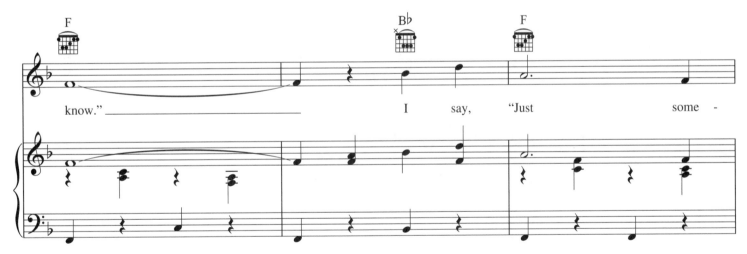

know." _____ I say, "Just some -

one ___ I used ___ to know." _____

LOOK AT US

Words and Music by MAX D. BARNES
and VINCE GILL

Look __ at __ us, ____ still __ lean - ing __ on _____ each __
Look __ at __ us, ____ still be - liev - ing __ in _____ for -

__ oth - er. __
- ev - er. __

If you want to see _____ how true

love should be, ___ then just __ look at us.

Look at

In a hun - dred __ years from now, ___ I

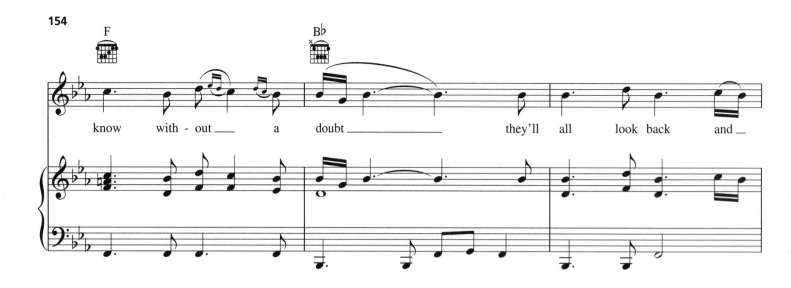

know with-out ___ a doubt ___ they'll all look back and ___

won - der ___ how ___ we made it ___ all work ___

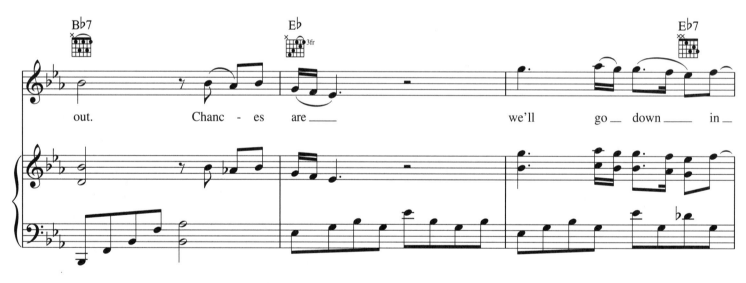

out. Chanc - es are ___ we'll go ___ down ___ in ___

___ his-to-ry. When they want to see how true

love should be, ___ they'll just ___ look at us.

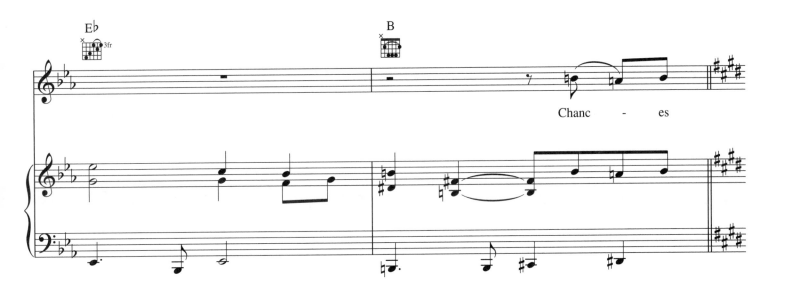

Chanc - es

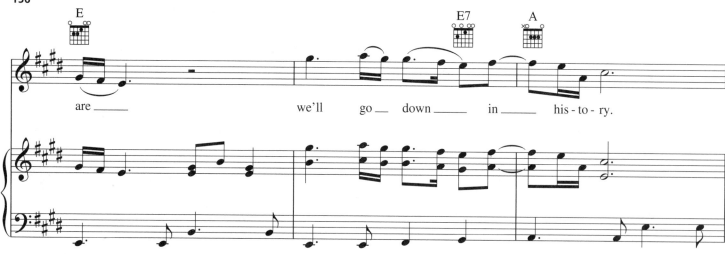

are _____ we'll go _ down _____ in _____ his - to - ry.

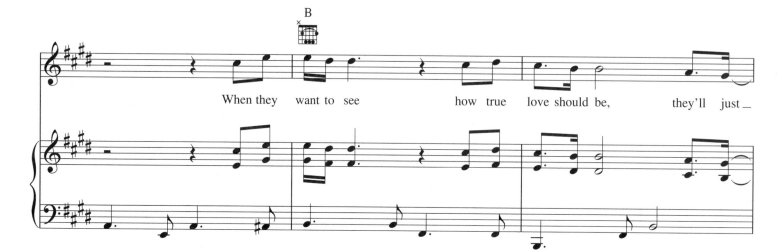

When they want to see how true love should be, they'll just _

_____ look at us. When they want to see _____ how true

love should be, _ they'll just _ look at us.

LOST IN THE FIFTIES TONIGHT
(In the Still of the Nite)

Words and Music by MIKE REID,
TROY SEALS and FRED PARRIS

Chorus

shared when _ they'd _ play: In the still of the

nite, ___ hold _ me, dar-ling, ____ hold _ me tight. ____ Oh, ____

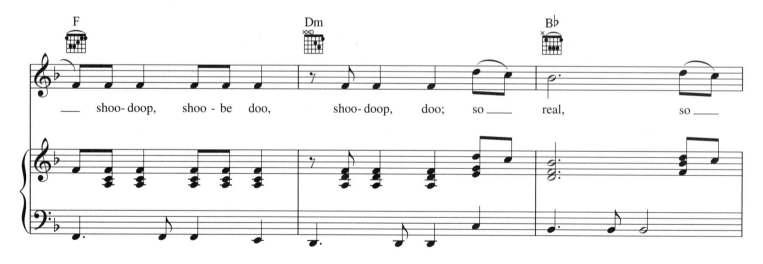

_ shoo-doop, shoo-be doo, shoo-doop, doo; so _ real, so _

right, lost in the fif-ties to-night.

Additional Lyrics

2. These precious hours, we know can't survive.
   Love's all that matters while the past is alive.
   Now and for always, till time disappears,
   We'll hold each other whenever we hear:
   Chorus

LOVE IS LIKE A BUTTERFLY

Words and Music by
DOLLY PARTON

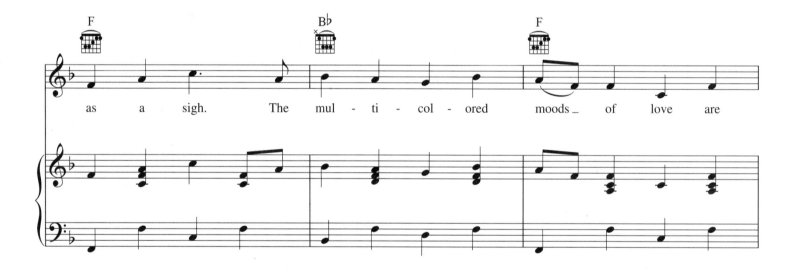

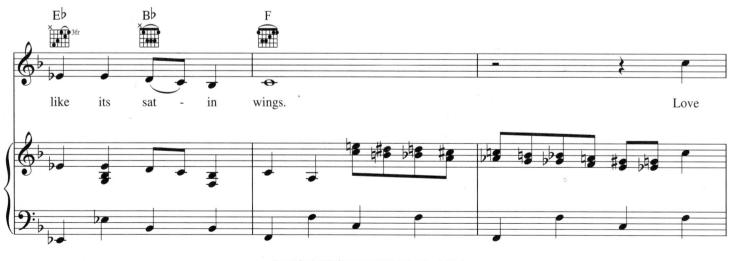

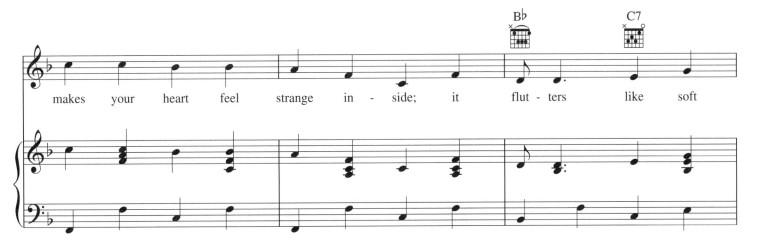

makes your heart feel strange in - side; it flut - ters like soft

wings in flight. Love is like _____ a but - ter - fly, a

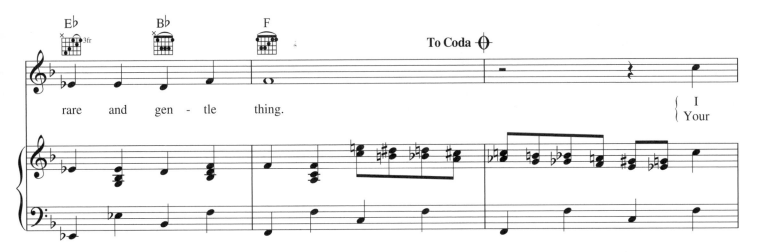

rare and gen - tle thing.

To Coda ⊕

I
Your

feel it when you're with me;
laugh - ter brings me sun - shine.

it hap - pens when you
Ev - 'ry day is

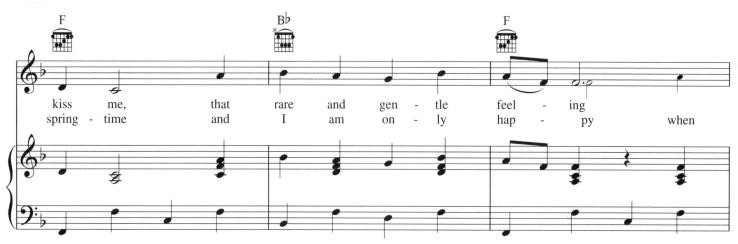

kiss me, that rare and gen - tle feel - ing
spring - time and I am on - ly hap - py when

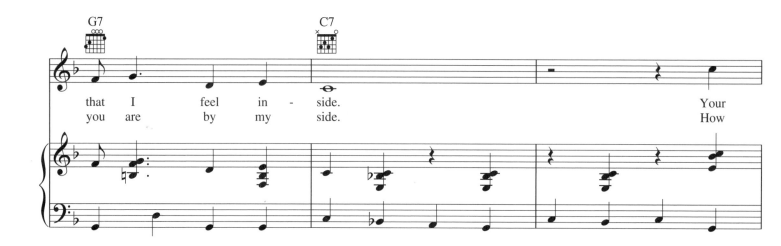

that I feel in - side. Your
you are by my side. How

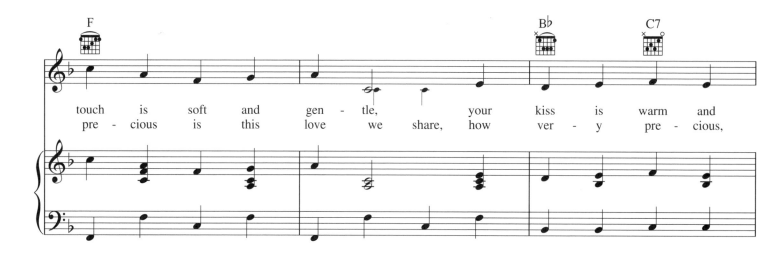

touch is soft and gen - tle, your kiss is warm and
pre - cious is this love we share, how ver - y pre - cious,

ten - der. When - ev - er I am with you, I ____
sweet and rare. __ To - geth - er we be - long like daf - fo -

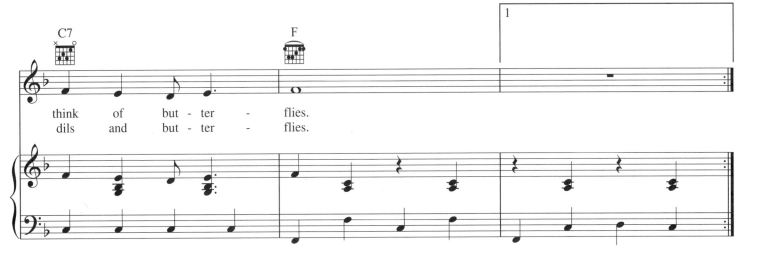

think of but-ter - flies.
dils and but-ter - flies.

D.C. al Coda

CODA

Love is like ___ a

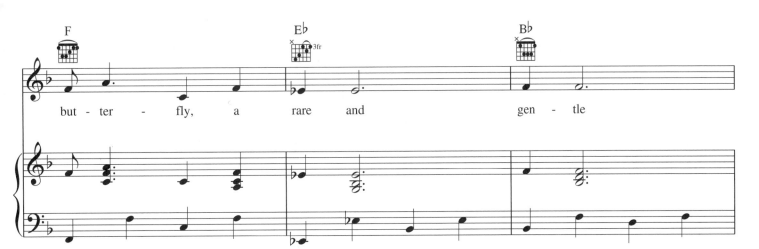

but - ter - fly, a rare and gen - tle

thing. _____

LOVESICK BLUES

Words by IRVING MILLS
Music by CLIFF FRIEND

tried and I tried ___ to keep her sat-is-fied, but she just would-n't

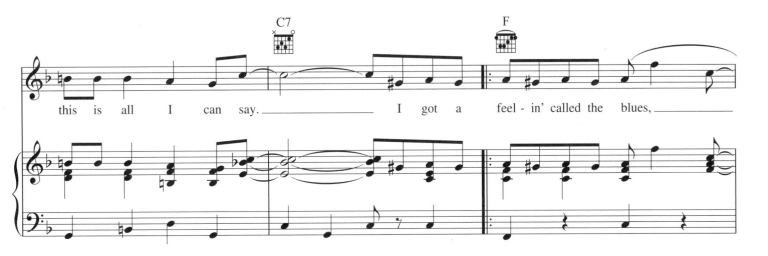

stay. So, now that she ___ is leav - in',

this is all I can say. ___ I got a feel-in' called the blues, ___

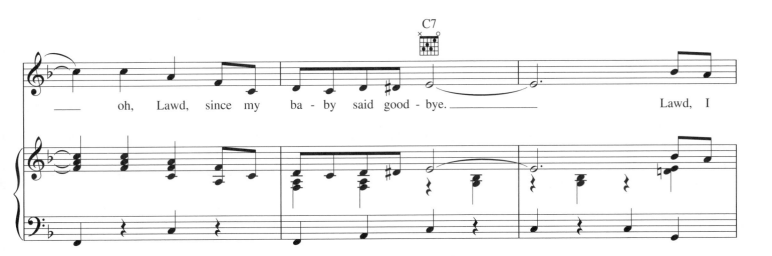

___ oh, Lawd, since my ba-by said good-bye. ___ Lawd, I

don't know what I'll do. _____ All I do is sit and sigh. _____ That last long

day she said good - bye, well, Lawd, I thought _ I would cry. ___ She'd

do me, she'd do you, she's got that kind of lov - in'. Lawd, I love to hear her when she

calls me "Sweet Dad - dy." _____ Such a beau - ti - ful dream, _____

I hate to think it all o - ver. I've lost my heart, it seems.

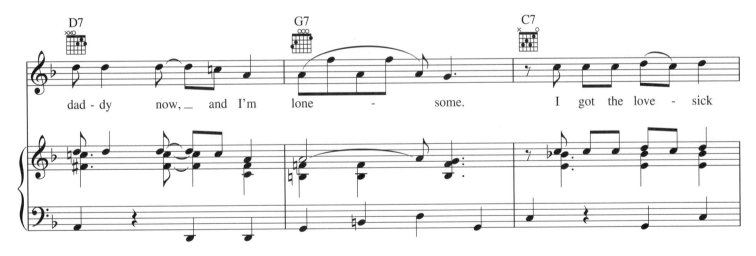

I've grown so used to you some - how. Lawd, I'm no - bod - y's sug - ar

dad - dy now, and I'm lone - some. I got the love - sick

blues. I got a blues.

MAKE THE WORLD GO AWAY

Words and Music by
HANK COCHRAN

MAKING BELIEVE

Words and Music by
JIMMY WORK

Moderate Country

Mak - ing be - lieve _____ that you ___ still
lieve _____ that I nev - er

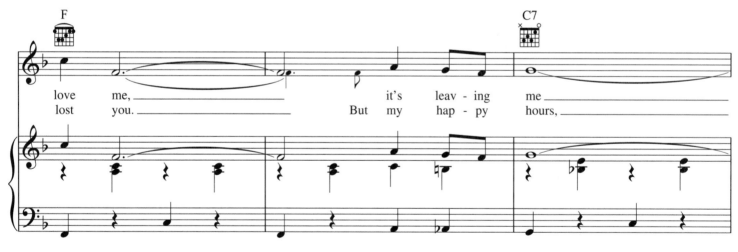

love me, _____ it's leav - ing me _____
lost you. _____ But my hap - py hours, _____

___ a - lone and so blue. _____ But I'll al - ways
___ I find, are so few. _____ My plans for the

dream, _____ still I'll nev - er own you. _____
fu - ture _____ will nev - er come true. _____

__ Mak - ing be - lieve, _____ it's all I can do. _____
__ Mak - ing be - lieve, _____ what else can I do? _____

__ Can't hold you close _____ when you're _ not

with me. _____ You're some - bod - y's love, _____

MAYBE IT WAS MEMPHIS

Words and Music by
MICHAEL ANDERSON

Slowly, but steadily

mf

Look-in' at you through a mist-y moon-light, ka-ty-did sing like a sym-pho-ny. ___
Read a-bout you in a Faulk-ner nov-el. Met you once in a Wil-liams play. ___
Ev-'ry night now since ___ I've been back home, lie a-wake, drift-ing in my mem-o-ry. ___

Porch swing sway-in' like a Ten-nes-see lull-a-by, mel-o-dy blow-ing through the wil-low tree. ___
Heard a-bout you ___ in a coun-try love song, sum-mer night beau-ty took my breath a-way. ___
Think a-bout you on my ma-ma's front porch swing talk-ing that way so soft to me. ___

What was I s'posed to do? ___ Stand-in' there look-in' at you,

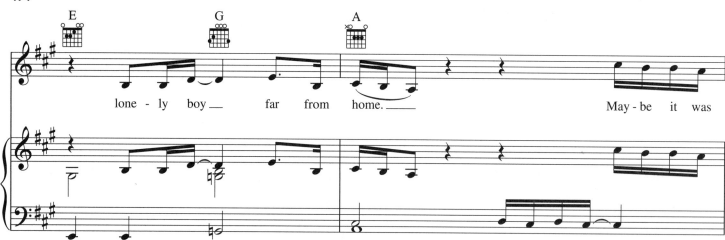

lone - ly boy ___ far from home. ___ May - be it was

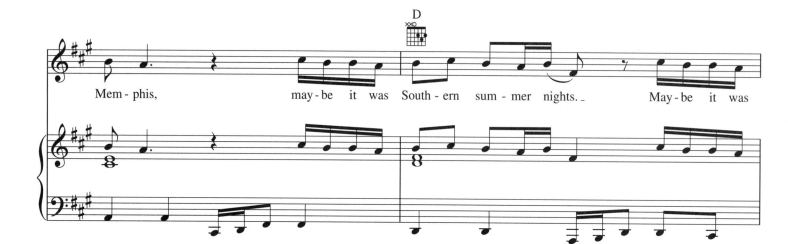

Mem - phis, may - be it was South - ern sum - mer nights. _ May - be it was

you, may - be it was me, but it sure felt right. ___

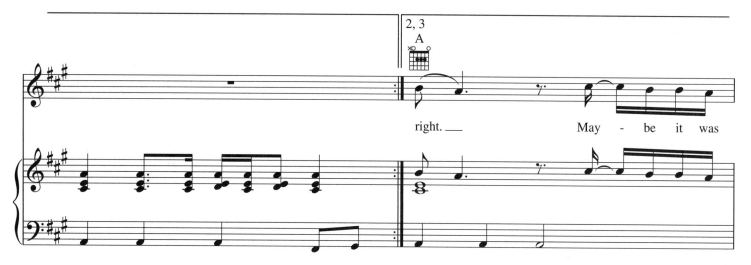

right. ___ May - be it was

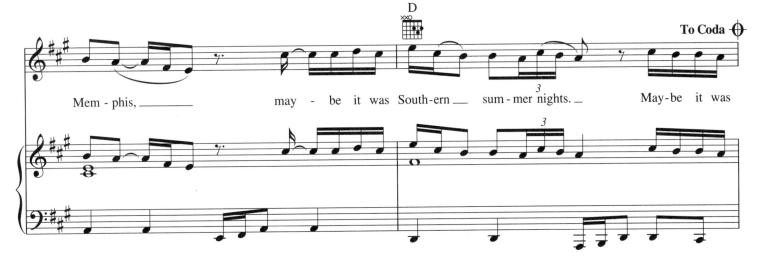

To Coda

Mem - phis, _____ may - be it was South - ern _____ sum - mer nights. _____ May-be it was

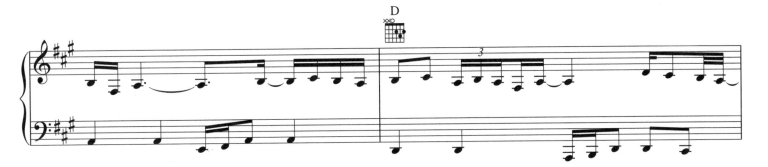

Bm7   D   A

you, _ may - be it was me, but it sure felt right. _____

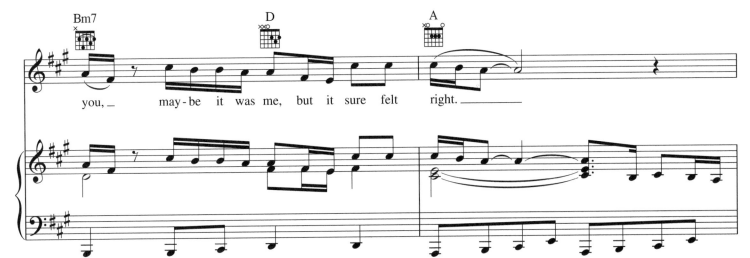

D

Bm7   D   A

D   Bm7   D   A

D.S. al Coda

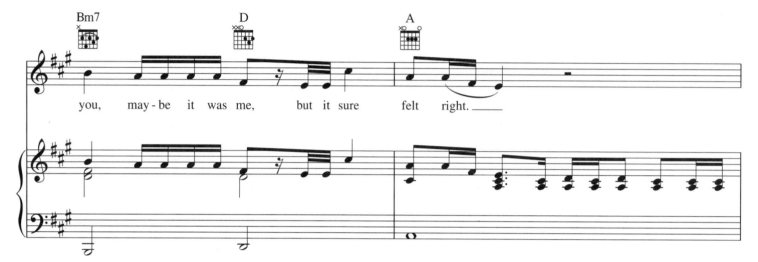

MY WOMAN MY WOMAN MY WIFE

Words and Music by
MARTY ROBBINS

too man-y hours in the sun.
smiles when I want to stop.

Eyes that show some dis-ap-
Lips that are wea - ry, but

point - ment, _____ and there's been quite a lot in her life.
ten - der _____ with love that strength - ens my life.

But
A

she's the foun-da - tion I lean on, _____
saint in a dress made of ging - ham, _____

my wom-an, my wom-an, my

wife.

Two lit-tle ba-bies were born in the spring, but

died when the win- ter was new.   I lost con- trol of my

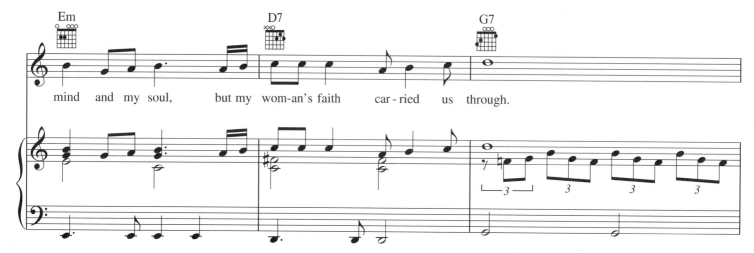

mind and my soul,   but my wom-an's faith   car- ried   us through.

When she reach- es   that   riv - er, _____   Lord,   you know   what she's

worth,   give   her that man-sion   up   yon- der, _____   'cause she's

been through hell here on earth. Lord, give her my share of

heav- en, _____ if I've earned an- y here in this life. 'Cause,

God, I be-lieve she de- serves it, my wom- an, my

wom- an, my wife. _____

NOW THAT I FOUND YOU

Words and Music by PAUL BEGAUD,
J.D. MARTIN and VANESSA CORISH

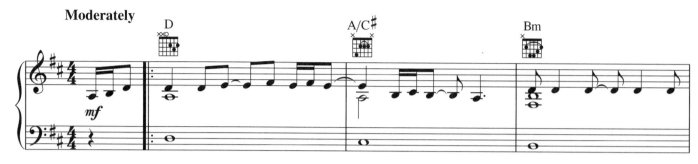

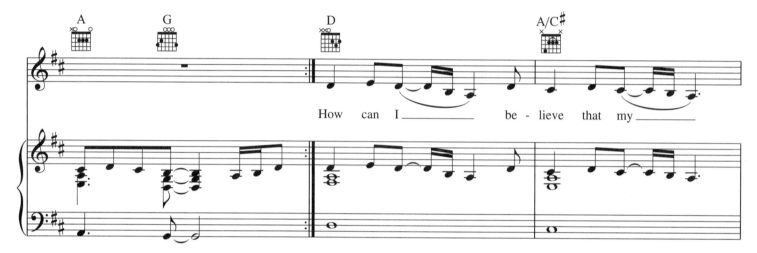

How can I _____ be-lieve that my _____ heart would find _____ some-one _____ like you. _____ You see _____ the

real _____ me, _____ no in-be-tweens, _____ I have no-where _____ to hide.

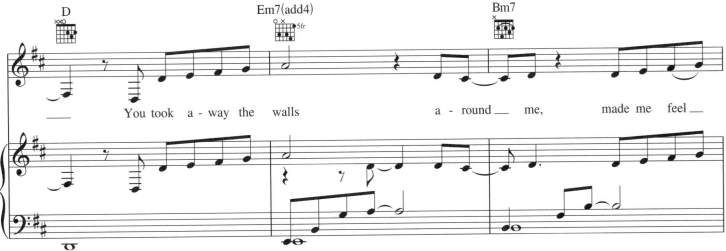

You took a - way the walls a - round __ me, made me feel __

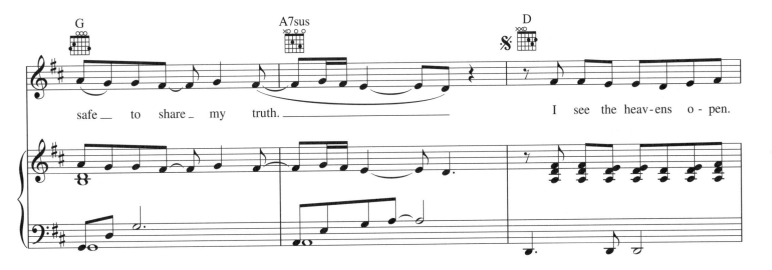

safe __ to share __ my truth. _____ I see the heav-ens o - pen.

A heart that once was bro - ken is hold - in' noth - in' back now that I found you. _

__ You hold me like a prayer, __ you touch me ev - 'ry - where. __ A life-time just ain't e - nough __

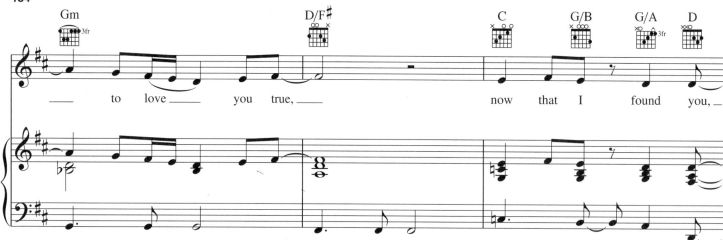

to love _____ you true, _____ now that I found you, _____

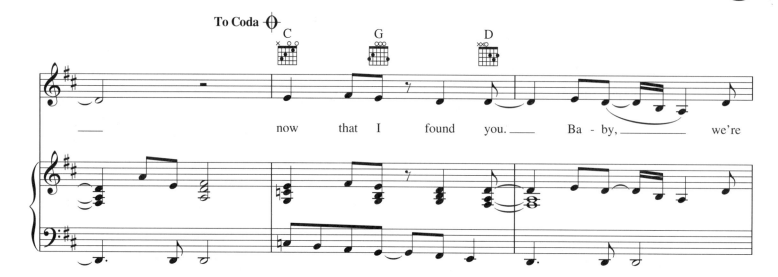

To Coda ⊕

_____ now that I found you. _____ Ba - by, _____ we're

meant to be, _____ a chem - is - try. _____ We'll last for - ev - er and

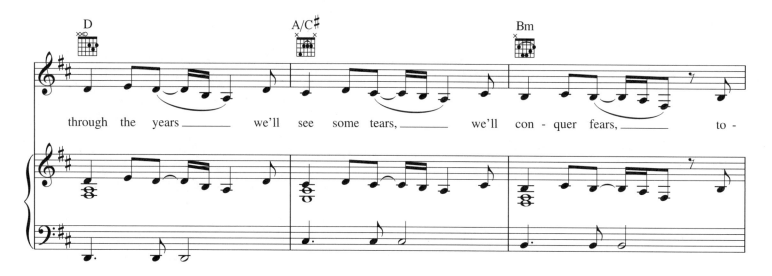

through the years _____ we'll see some tears, _____ we'll con - quer fears, _____ to -

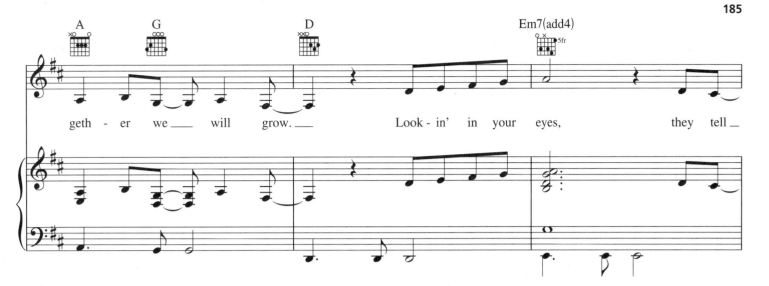

geth - er we __ will grow. __ Look - in' in your eyes, they tell __

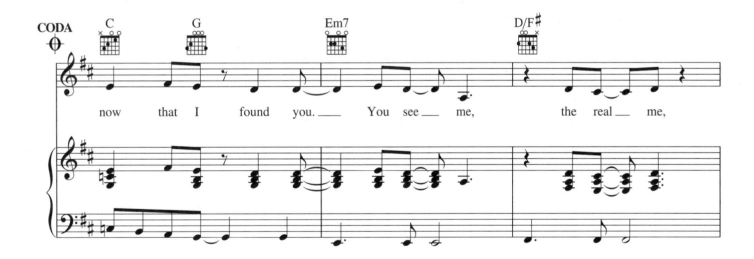

__ me I no long - er have __ to feel __ a - lone. __

D.S. al Coda

CODA

now that I found you. __ You see __ me, the real __ me,

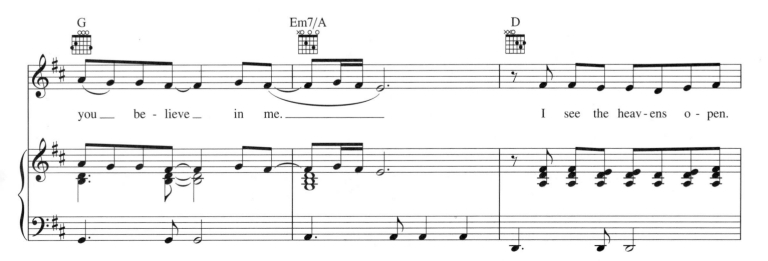

you __ be - lieve __ in me. __ I see the heav - ens o - pen.

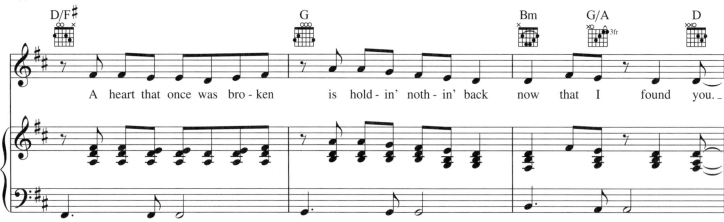

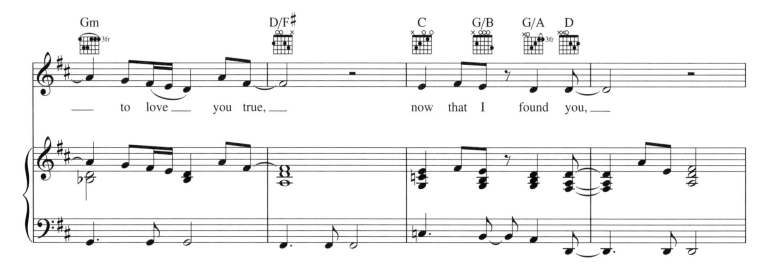

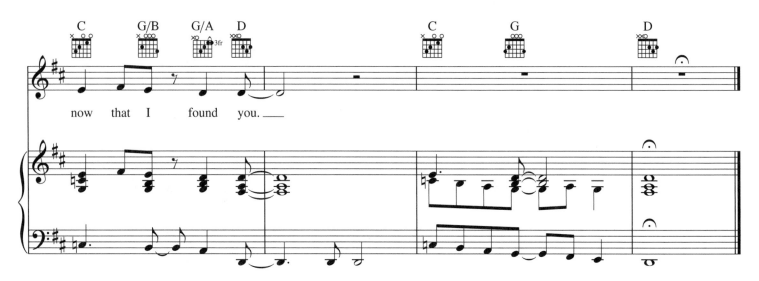

OH, LONESOME ME

Words and Music by
DON GIBSON

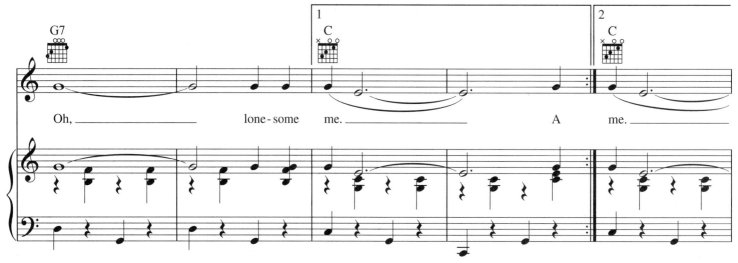

Oh, _____ lone-some me. _____ A me. _____

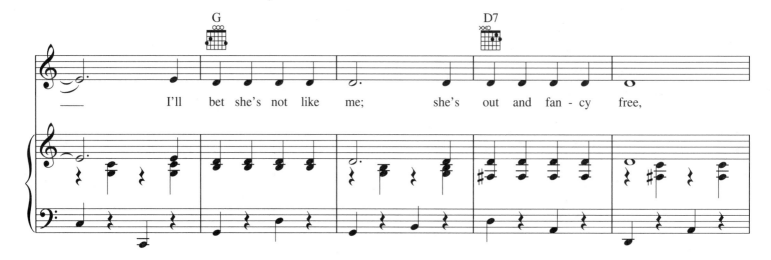

_____ I'll bet she's not like me; she's out and fan-cy free,

flirt-ing with the boys with all her charms. _____ But I still love her

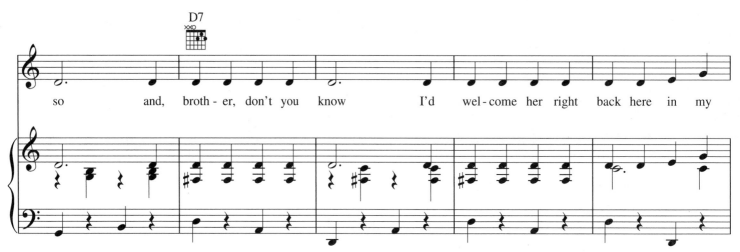

so and, broth-er, don't you know I'd wel-come her right back here in my

arms. _____ Well, there must be some way I can lose these lone-some blues, ___

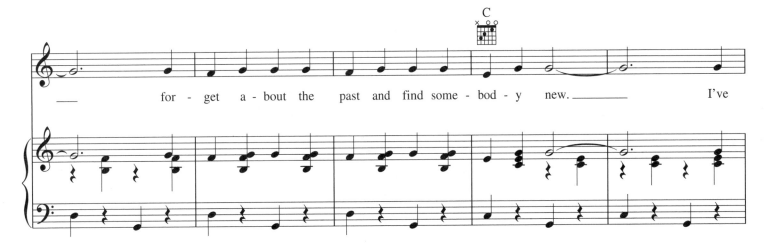

for - get a - bout the past and find some - bod - y new. _____ I've

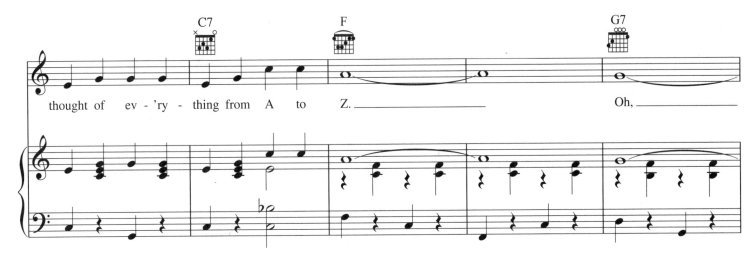

thought of ev - 'ry - thing from A to Z. _____ Oh, _____

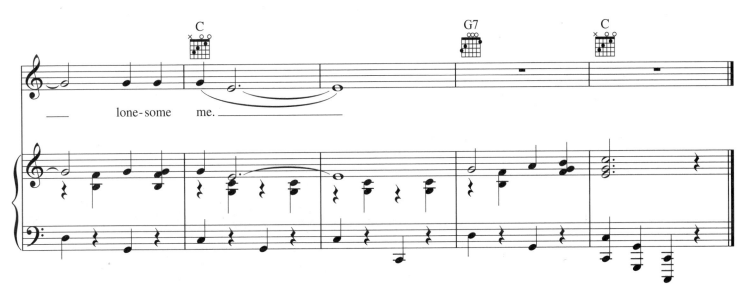

lone - some me. _____

ONCE A DAY

Words and Music by
BILL ANDERSON

Moderately fast

When you found ____ some-bod - y new, ____ I thought I
I'm so glad ____ that I'm not like ____ a girl I

nev - er would _ for - get ____ you for
knew one time. ____ She lost ____ the one for she

I thought then ___ I nev - er could. ____ But time ____
loved and slow - ly lost ___ her mind. She ___

* Recorded a half step lower.

has tak - en all the pains _ a - way. Un - til now _
sat a - round and cried her life _ a - way. Luck - y me, _

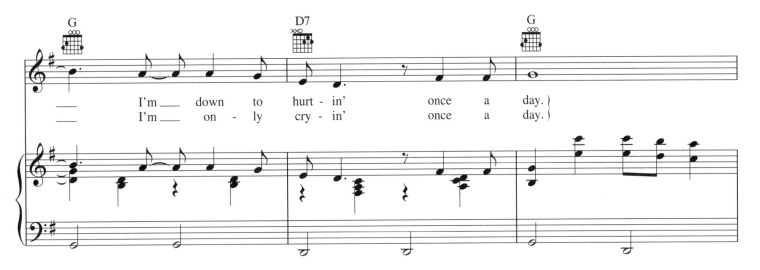

_ I'm _ down to hurt - in' once a day.
_ I'm _ on - ly cry - in' once a day.

Once a day, all day long

and once _ a night from dusk till dawn,

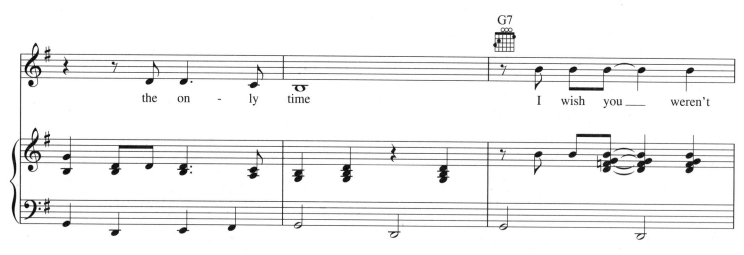

the on - ly time

I wish you ___ weren't

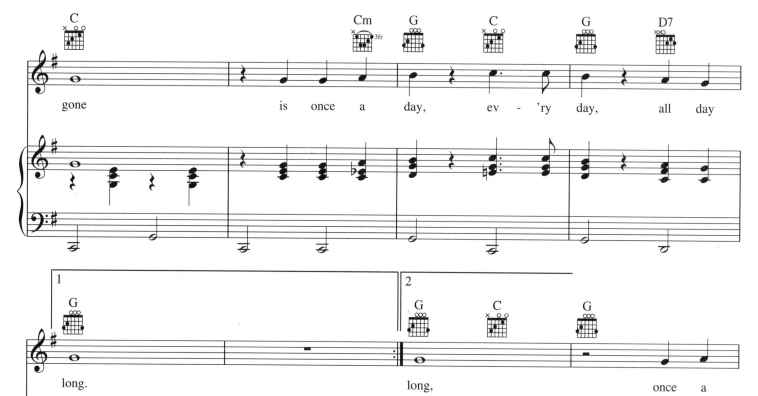

gone

is once a day, ev - 'ry day, all day

long.

long,

once a

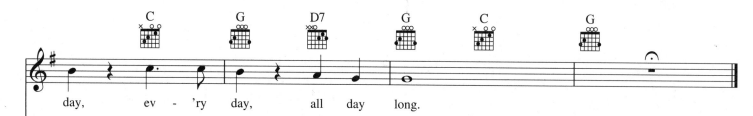

day, ev - 'ry day, all day long.

A ROSE AND A BABY RUTH

Words and Music by
JOHN D. LOUDERMILK

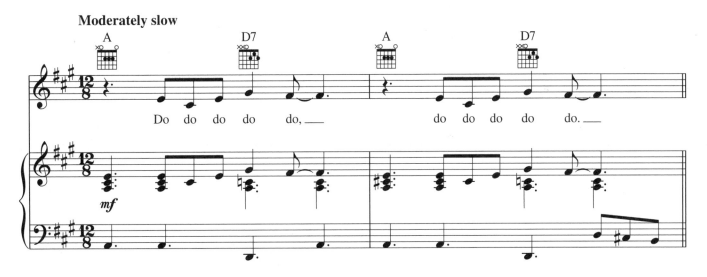

Do do do do do, ___ do do do do do. ___

We had a quar - rel, ___ a teen - age quar - rel. ___

Now I'm as blue _____ as I know how ___ to be.

I can't call you ____ on the phone.

I can't e - ven ____ see you ____ at your home.

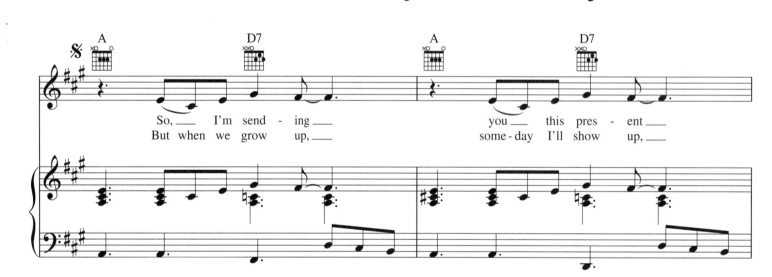

So, ____ I'm send - ing ____ you ____ this pres - ent ____
But when we grow up, ____ some - day I'll show up, ____

just ____ to prove ____ that I'm tell - ing ____ the truth.
just ____ to prove ____ I was tell - ing ____ the truth.

Dear, I be - lieve you won't laugh when you re-ceive } this rose and __ a Ba - by
I'll kiss you, too, then I'll hand _ to you }

Ruth. _____ Do do do do do, __ do do do do do. __

Ah. _____ I could have sent you __ an or - chid of some kind,

but that's all I had in ____ my jeans ____ at the time.

Ooh. _____

ONE MORE DAY
(With You)

Words and Music by STEVEN DALE JONES
and BOBBY TOMERLIN

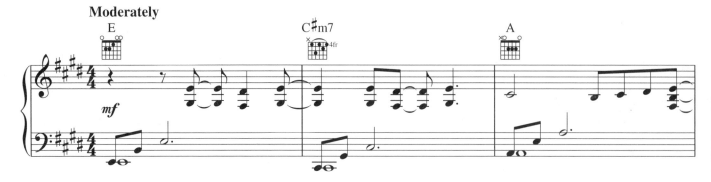

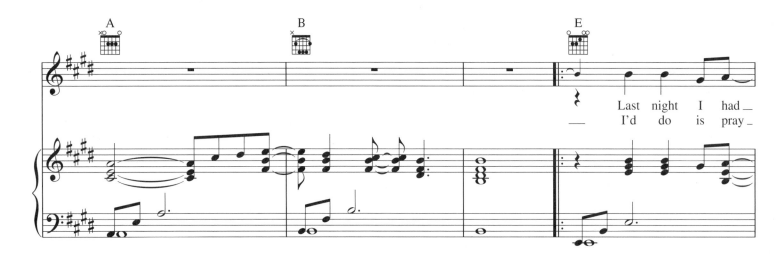

Last night I had ___
___ I'd do is pray ___

___ a cra-zy ___ dream.
___ for time ___ to ___ crawl.

wish was grant - ed just _____ for me. _____ It could be for an - y - thing.
I'd un - plug _ the tel - e - phone, _ keep the T _ V off. _____

_____ I did - n't ask for mon - ey _____ or a
_____ I'd hold _____ you ev - 'ry sec - ond, say a

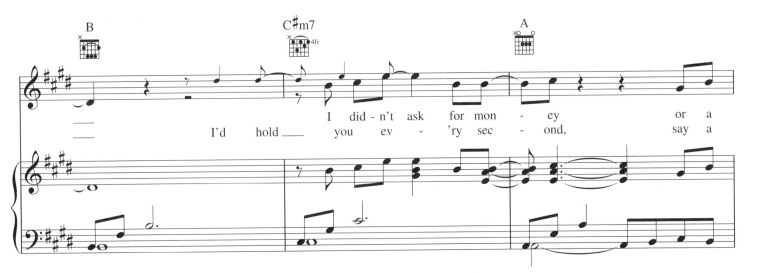

man - sion on Mal - i - bu. _____ I sim - ply wished _ for
mil - lion "I _____ love you's." _____ It's what I'd do _____ with

one more day _ with you. _
one more day _ with you. _ }   One _ more day, _____

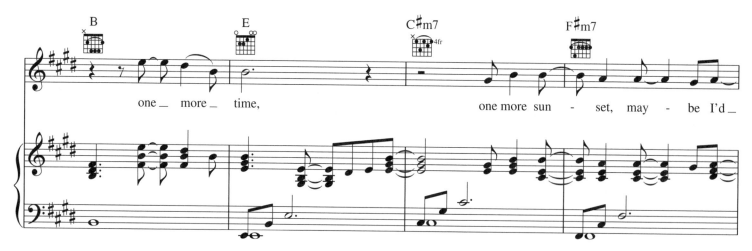

one __ more __ time, one more sun - set, may - be I'd __

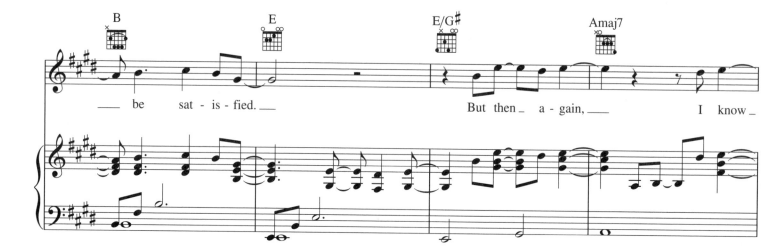

__ be sat - is - fied. __ But then __ a - gain, ___ I know __

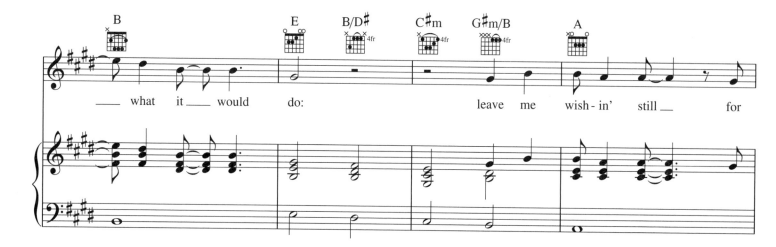

__ what it __ would do: leave me wish - in' still __ for

one more day __ with you. __

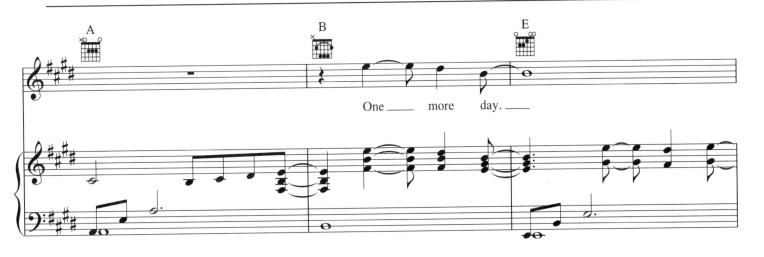

One ___ more day. ___

First thing ___

One ___ more day, ___

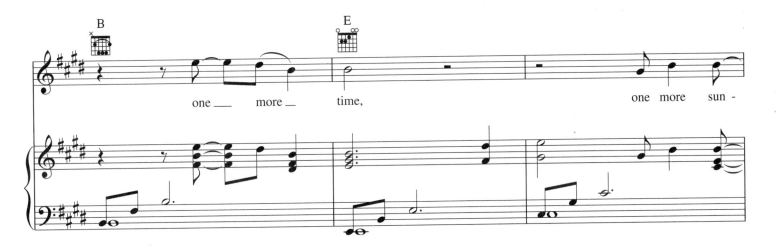

one ___ more ___ time,   one more sun -

- set, may - be I'd _____ be sat - is - fied. _____

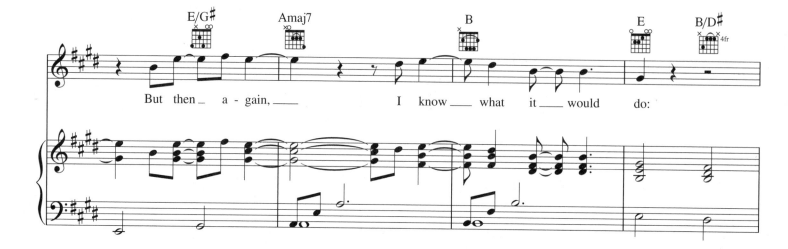

But then _ a - gain, _____ I know _____ what it _____ would do:

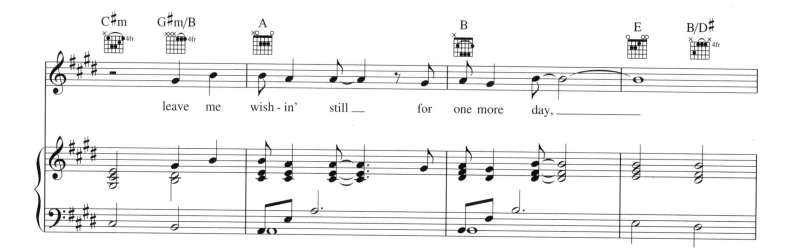

leave me wish - in' still __ for one more day, _____

leave me wish - in' still __ for one more day, _____

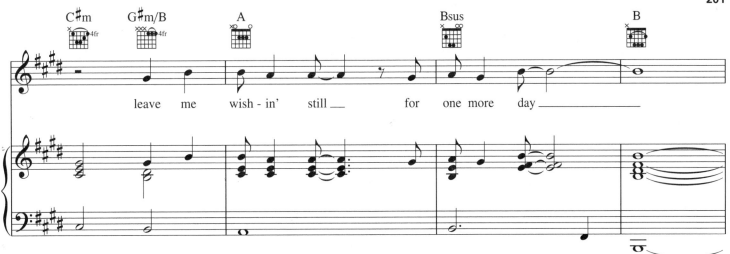

leave me wish-in' still ___ for one more day ___

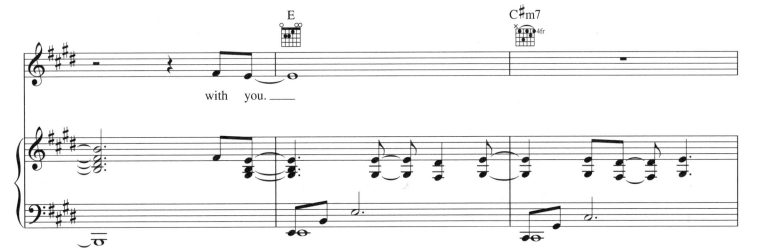

with you. ___

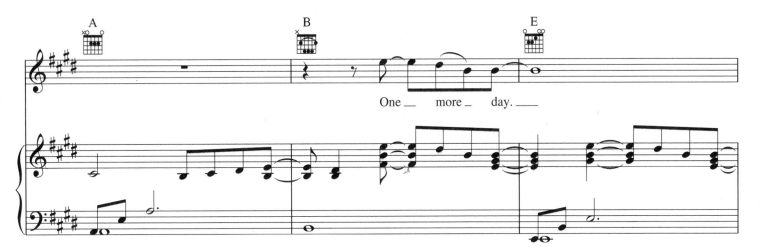

One ___ more ___ day. ___

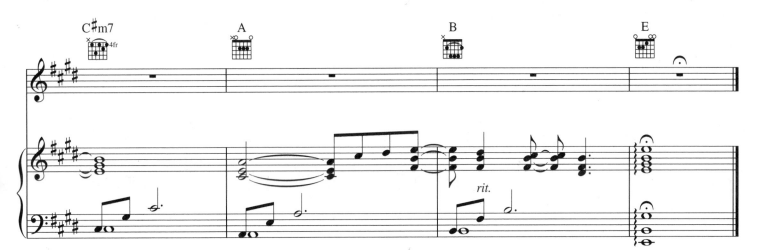

PLEASE HELP ME, I'M FALLING
(In Love with You)

Words and Music by DON ROBERTSON
and HAL BLAIR

PURE LOVE

Words and Music by
EDDIE RABBITT

Pure _____ love. _____ Ba - by, it's

pure _____ love. _____ Milk and hon - ey and Cap - tain

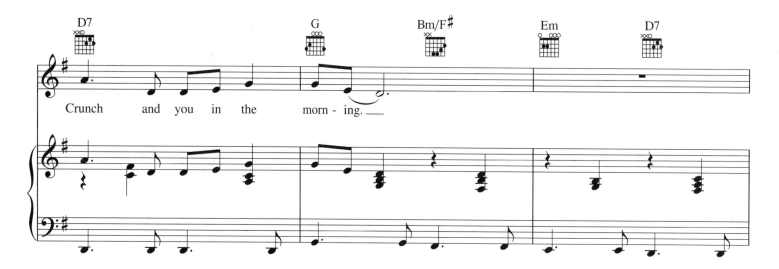

Crunch and you in the morn - ing. ___

blue-birds sing-in' right out - side my win - dow.

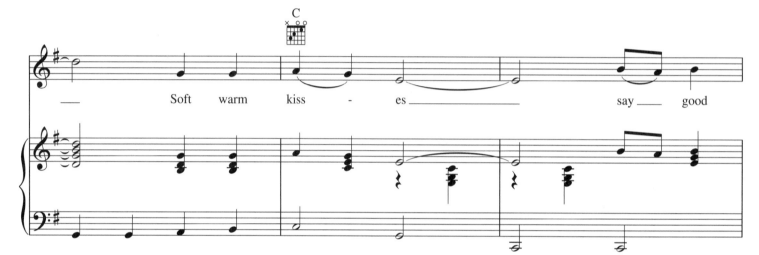

Soft warm kiss - es say good

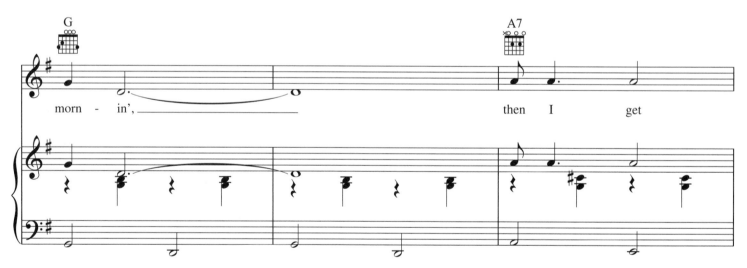

morn - in', then I get

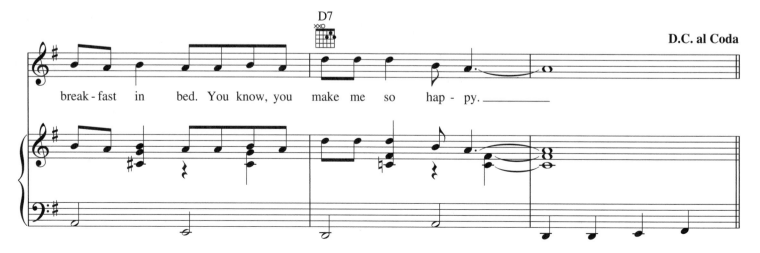

D.C. al Coda

break-fast in bed. You know, you make me so hap-py.

RELEASE ME

Words and Music by ROBERT YOUNT,
EDDIE MILLER and DUB WILLIAMS

Please re - lease me, let me go, ___
I have found a new love, dear, ___
Please re - lease me, can't you see ___

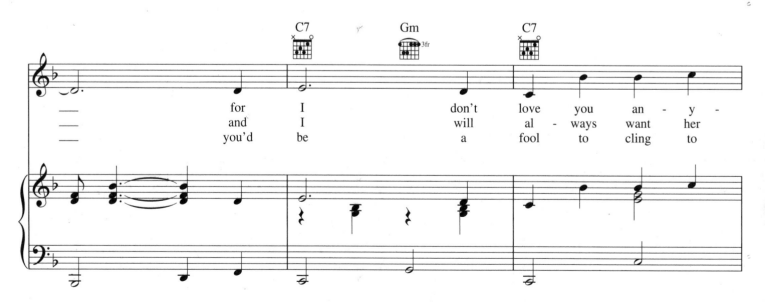

___ for I don't love you an - y -
___ and I will al - ways want her
you'd be a fool to cling to

more. _____
near. _____
me? _____

To waste our lives would be a
Her lips are warm while yours are
To live a lie would bring us

sin; _____
cold; _____
pain, _____

re - lease me and let me love a -
re - lease me, my dar - ling, let me
so re - lease me and let me love a -

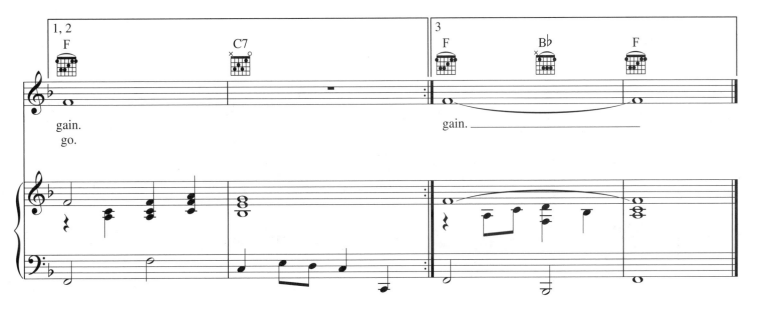

gain.
go.

gain. _____

REMEMBER WHEN

Words and Music by
ALAN JACKSON

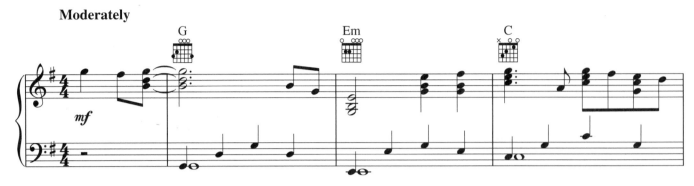

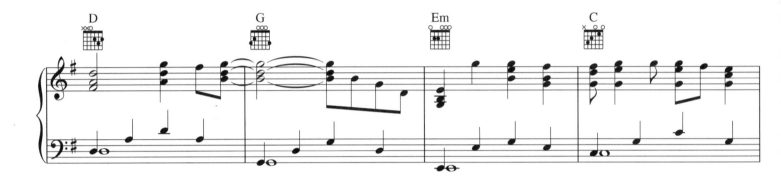

Re-mem-ber when ___
I was young ___
we vowed the vows ___

___ and so ___ were you   and time stood still ___   and
___ and walked ___ the walk   and gave our hearts, ___   made the start ___

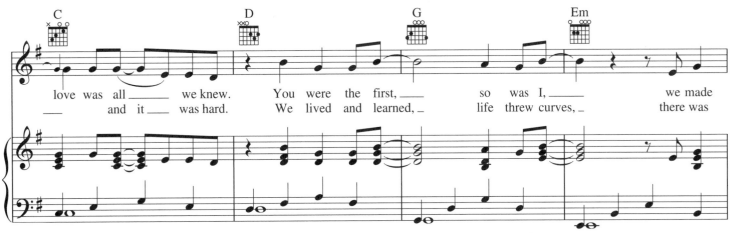

love was all _____ we knew. You were the first, _____ so was I, _____ we made
___ and it ___ was hard. We lived and learned, _ life threw curves, _ there was

love _ and then _ you cried. _____ Re-mem - ber when? _
joy _ and there _ was hurt. _____ Re-mem - ber when? _

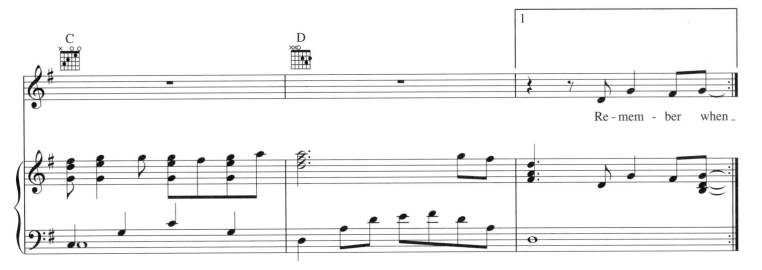

Re - mem - ber when _

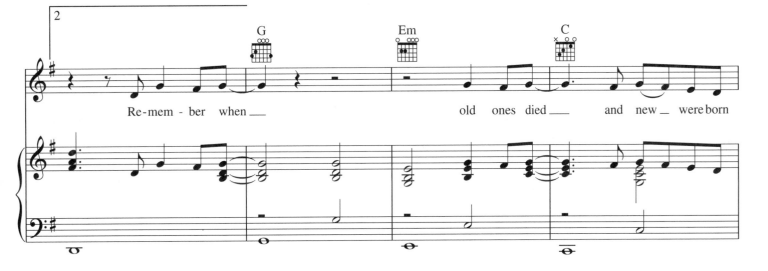

Re - mem - ber when _____ old ones died _____ and new _ were born

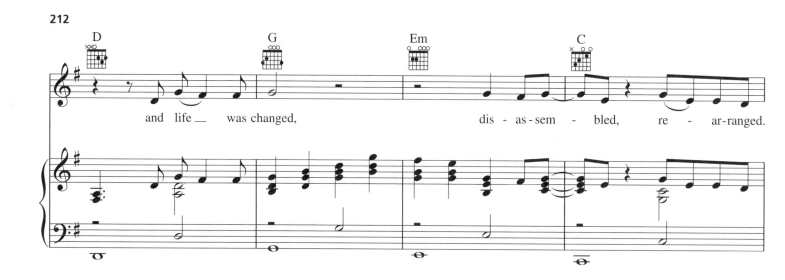

and life __ was changed, dis - as - sem - bled, re - ar-ranged.

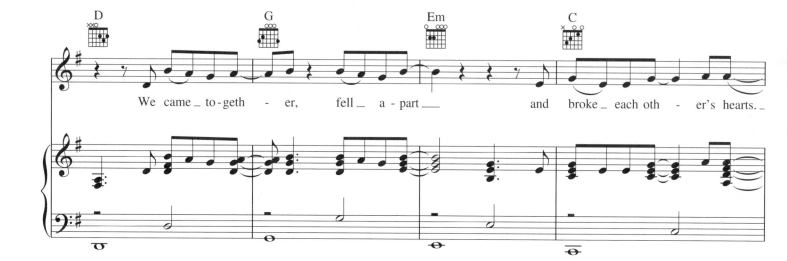

We came __ to-geth - er, fell __ a - part __ and broke __ each oth - er's hearts. __

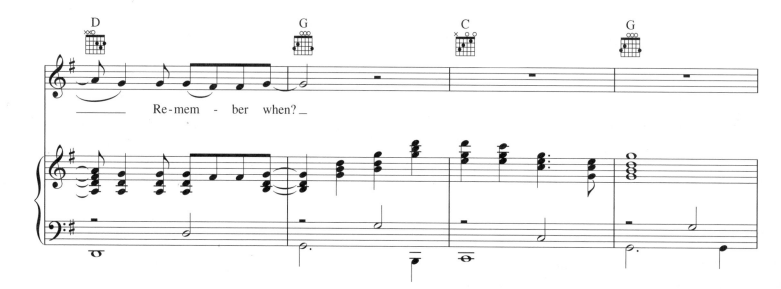

__ Re-mem - ber when? __

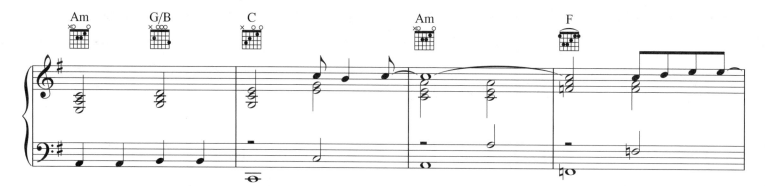

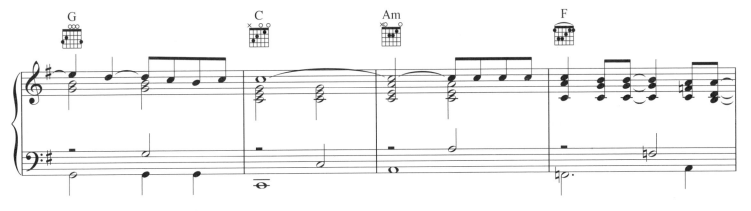

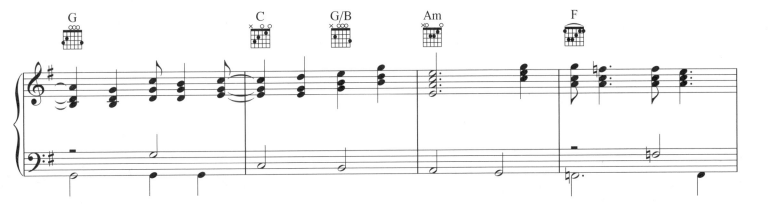

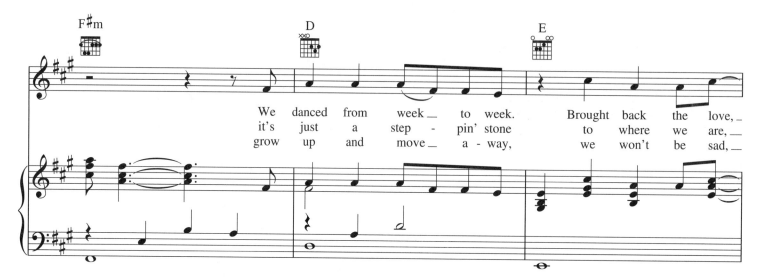

Re - mem - ber when _

D.S. al Coda

Re - mem - ber when _

CODA

and we'll re - mem - ber when,

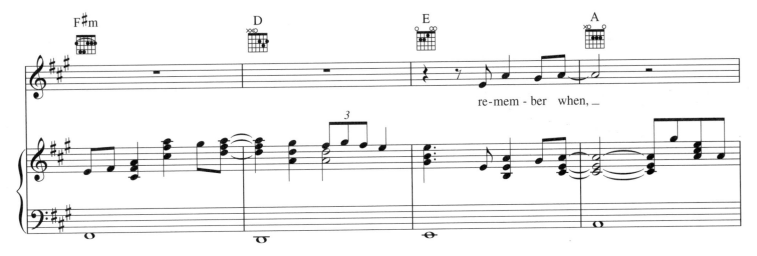

re - mem - ber when, _

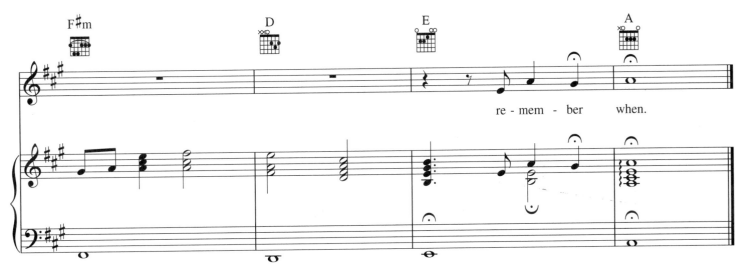

re - mem - ber when.

RING OF FIRE

Words and Music by MERLE KILGORE
and JUNE CARTER

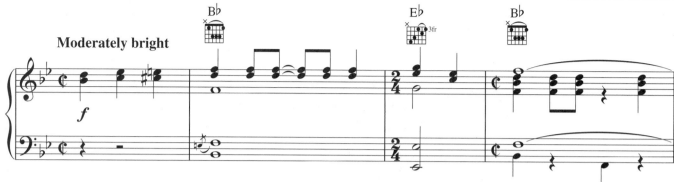

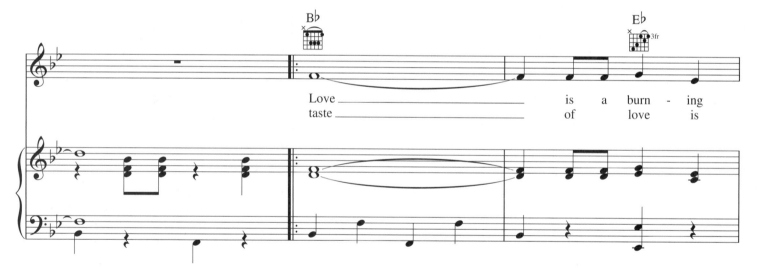

Love _____ is a burn-ing
taste _____ of love is

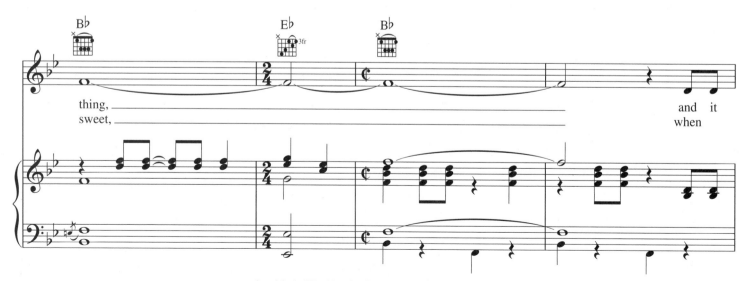

thing, _____ and it
sweet, _____ when

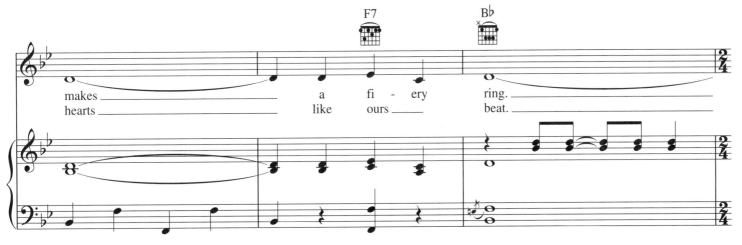

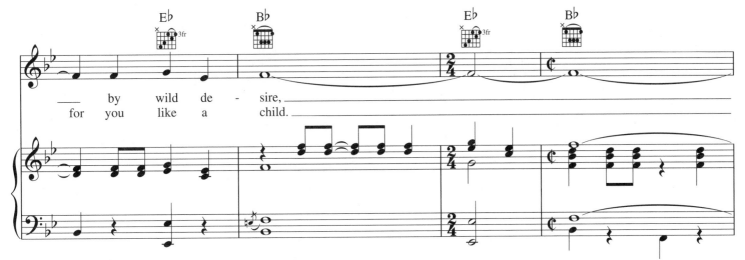

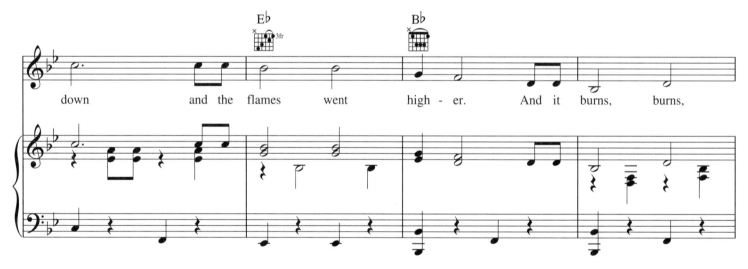

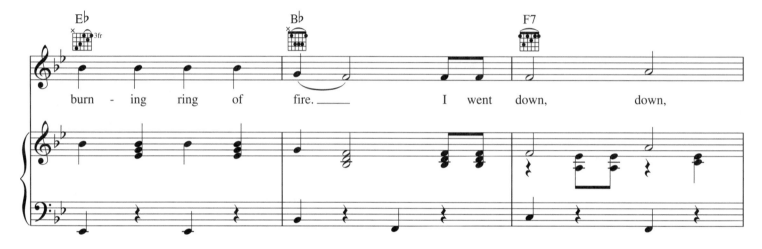

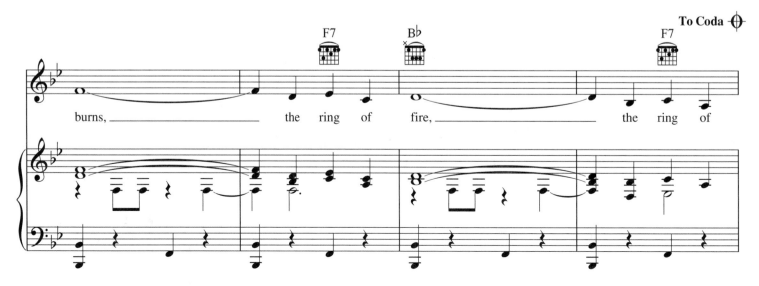

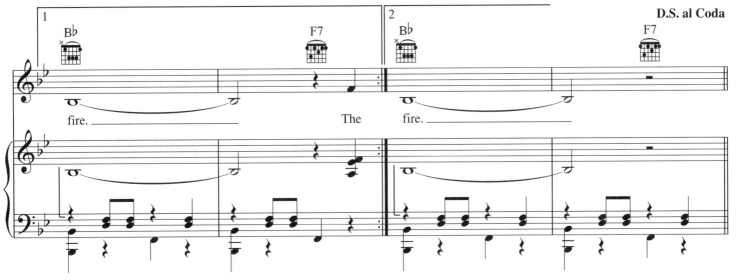

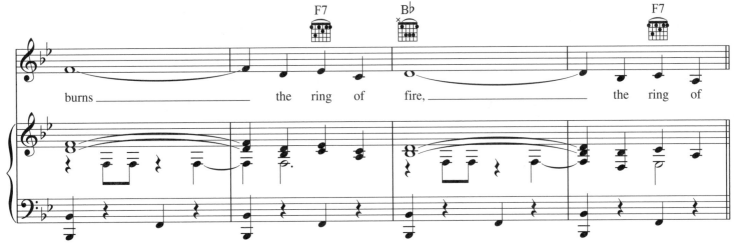

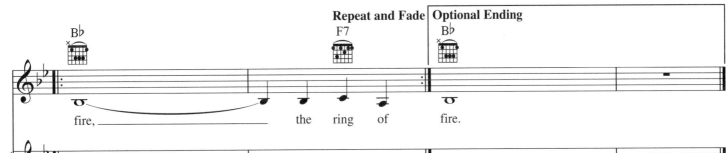

SEND ME THE PILLOW YOU DREAM ON

Words and Music by
HANK LOCKLIN

Send me the pil - low ___ that you dream on, ___

___ so, dar - ling, I can dream on it

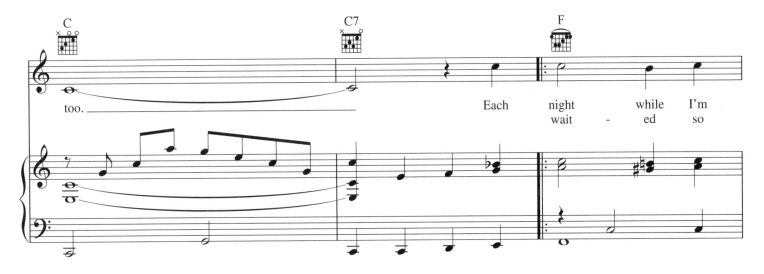

too. ___ Each night while I'm
wait - ed so

sleep - ing, oh, so lone - ly, ___ I'll
long for you to write me, ___ but

SHE'S EVERY WOMAN

Words and Music by VICTORIA SHAW
and GARTH BROOKS

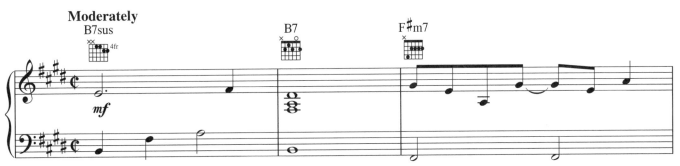

She's sun and rain, ____ she's fire and ice, ____ a lit - tle
and in L. A. ____ and ev - 'ry

cra - zy, but ____ it's nice. ____ And when she gets mad, ____ you best ____
town a - long ____ the way. ____ And she's ev - 'ry place ____

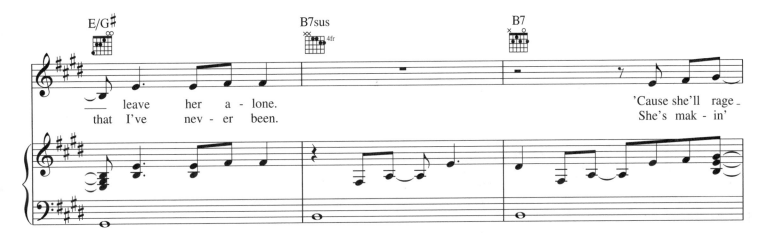

____ leave her a - lone. 'Cause she'll rage ____
that I've nev - er been. She's mak - in'

just like ___ a riv - er, then she'll beg you to ___ for - give ___
love on rain - y nights. _____ She's a stroll through Christ - mas lights. __

___ her. Oh, ___ she's ev - 'ry wom - an that I've ev - er known.
___ And she's ev - 'ry - thing ___ I want to do a - gain.

1
She's so New York ___

2
And it needs ___
Though

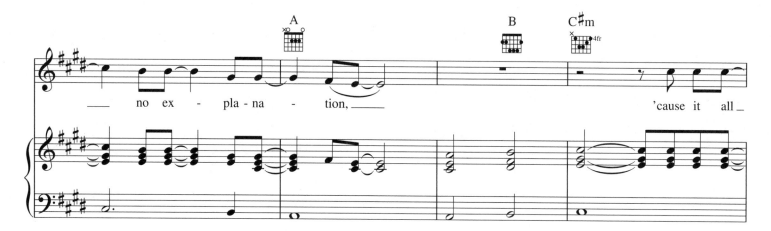

___ no ex - pla - na - tion, _____ 'cause it all ___

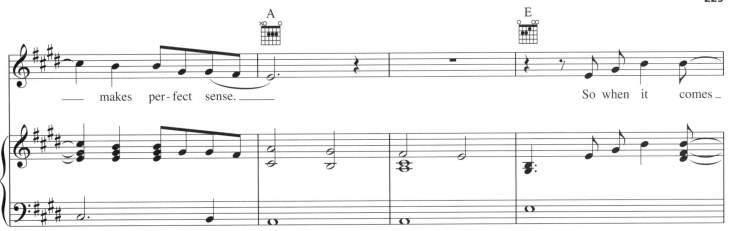

makes per-fect sense. _____ So when it comes _

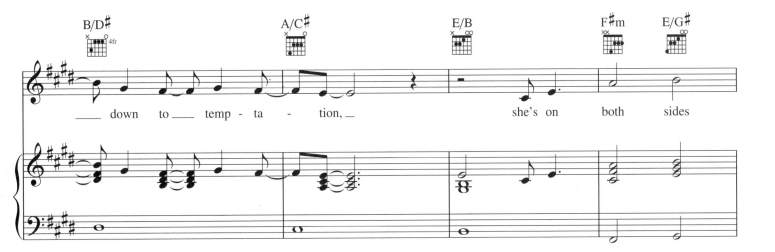

_____ down to _____ temp-ta - tion, _ she's on both sides

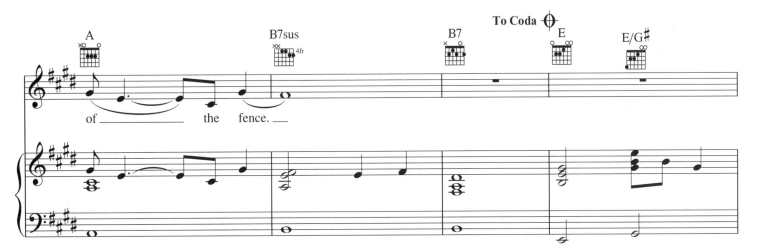

of _____ the fence. _

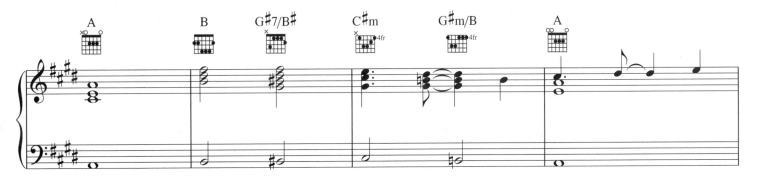

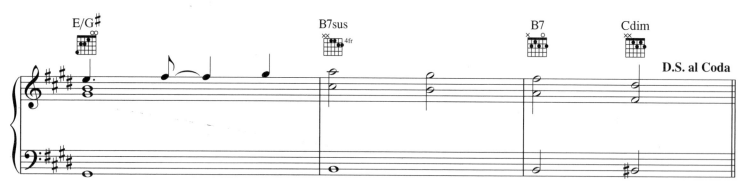

She's an - y - thing __ but typ - i - cal.

She's so un - pre - dict - a - ble. __ Oh, but e - ven at __ her worst,

she ain't __ that bad. __ She's as real __

as real __ can be _____ and she's ev - 'ry fan - ta - sy. __

Lord, __ she's ev - 'ry lov - er that I've ev - er had. __

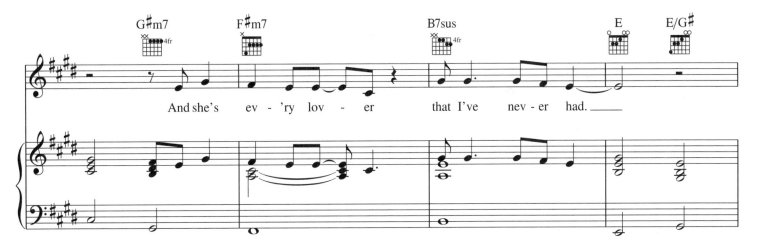

And she's ev - 'ry lov - er that I've nev - er had. __

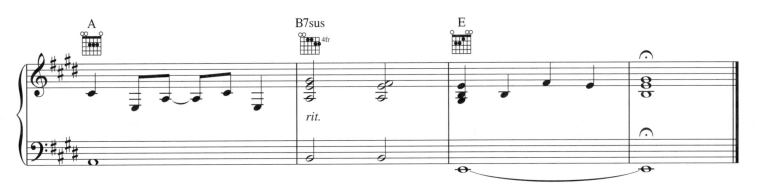

rit.

SHE THINKS I STILL CARE

Words and Music by
DICKEY LEE

229

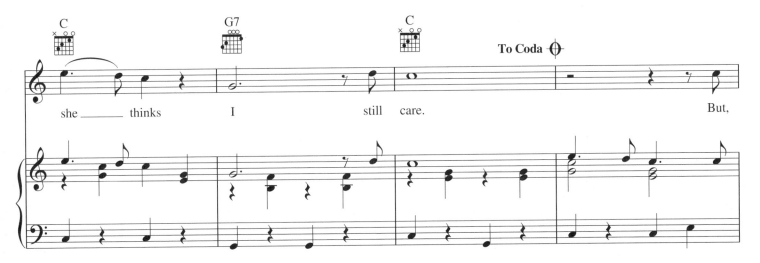

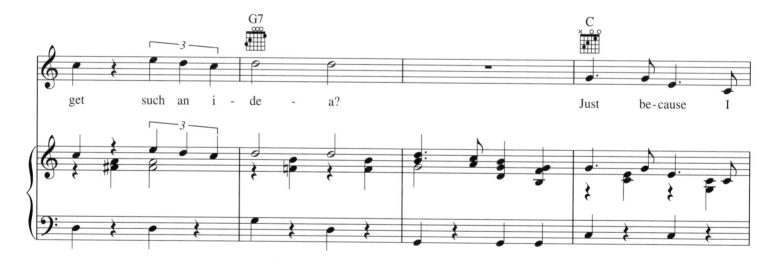

mem - 'ry _____ of her lin - gers _____ ev - 'ry - where, _____

D.S. al Coda

just be -

CODA

Just be - cause I saw her,

then went all to piec - es, _____

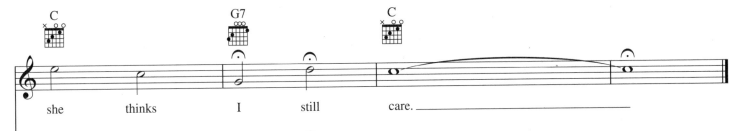

she thinks I still care. _____

SHE'S EVERYTHING

Words and Music by BRAD PAISLEY
and WIL NANCE

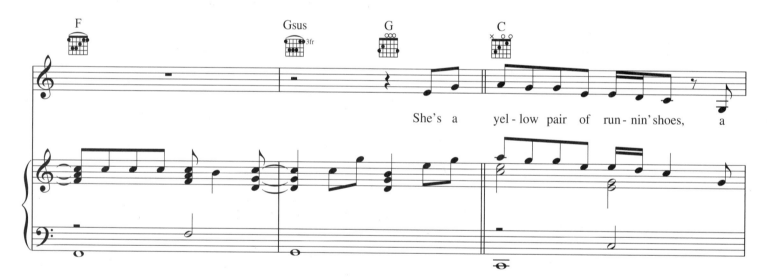

She's a yel-low pair of run-nin' shoes, a

hole-y pair of jeans. __ She looks great in cheap sun-glass-es, she looks

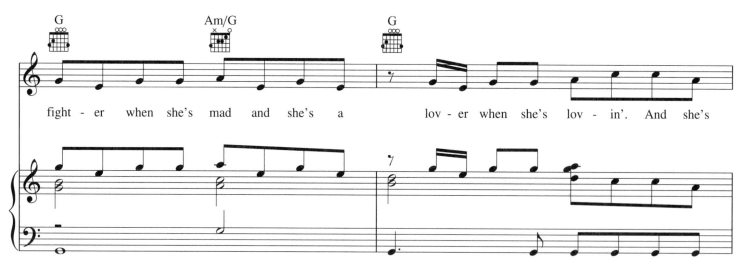

fight - er when she's mad and she's a lov - er when she's lov - in'. And she's

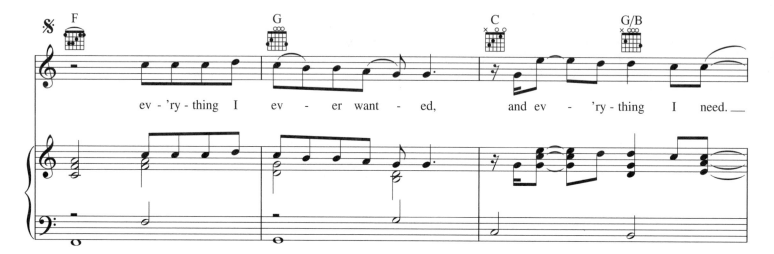

ev - 'ry - thing I ev - er want - ed, and ev - 'ry - thing I need. __

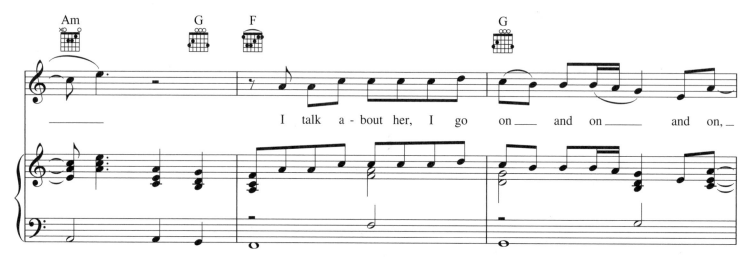

__ I talk a - bout her, I go on __ and on __ and on, __

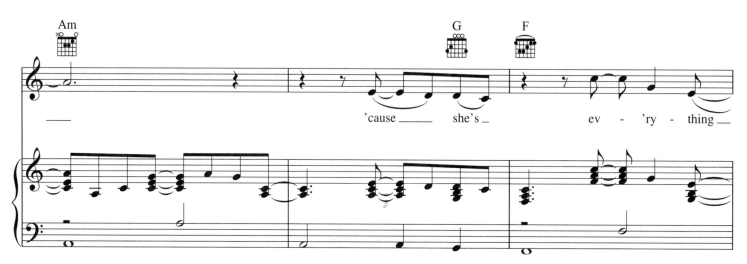

__ 'cause __ she's __ ev - 'ry - thing __

to me.

She's a Sat-ur-day out on the town and a

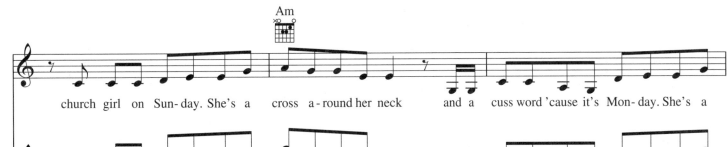

church girl on Sun-day. She's a cross a-round her neck and a cuss word 'cause it's Mon-day. She's a

bub-ble bath and can-dles, ba-by, come and kiss me. She's a one glass of wine and she's

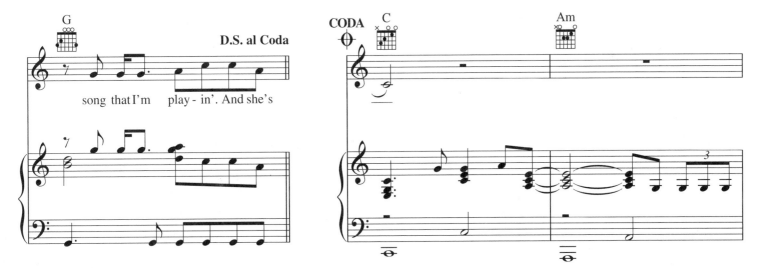

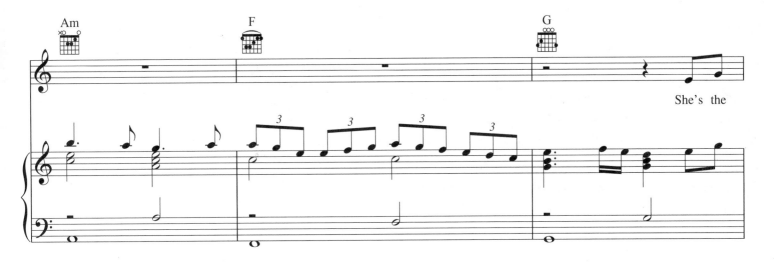

rock - in' right be - side me. Ev - 'ry day __ that pass - es I on - ly love her more. __

Yeah, she's the one __ that I'd lay down my own life for. And she's

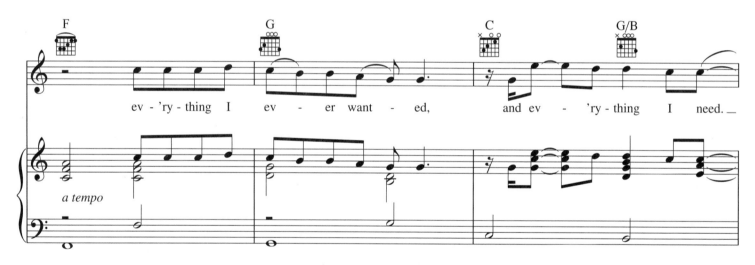

ev - 'ry - thing I ev - er want - ed, and ev - 'ry - thing I need. __

And she's ev - 'ry - thing __ to me. __

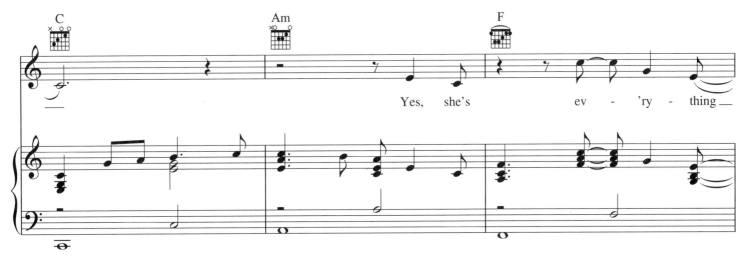

Yes, she's ev - 'ry - thing

to me.

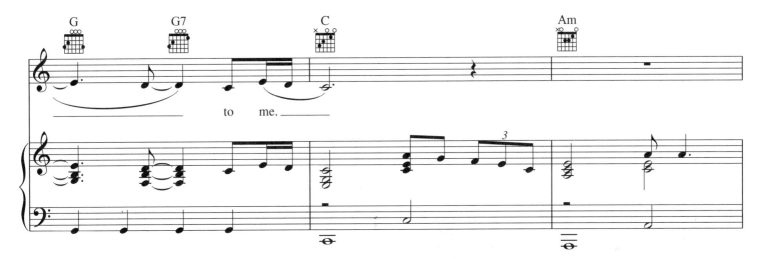

Ev - ry - thing I ev - er want - ed

and ev - 'ry - thing I need.

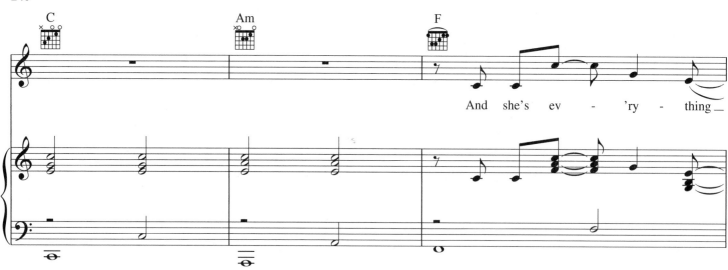

And she's ev - 'ry - thing

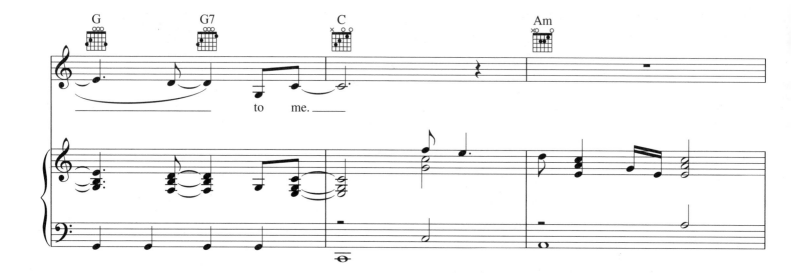

to me.

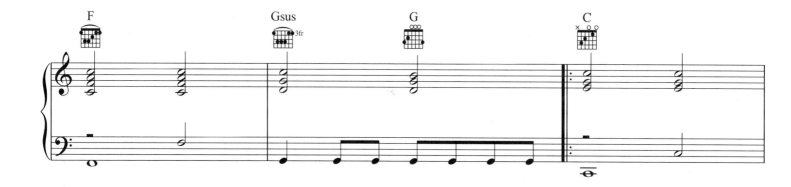

Repeat and Fade | **Optional Ending**

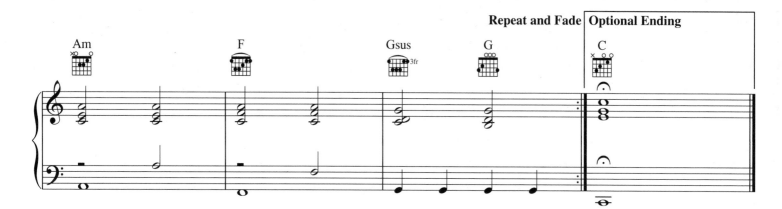

SHE'S GOT YOU

Words and Music by
HANK COCHRAN

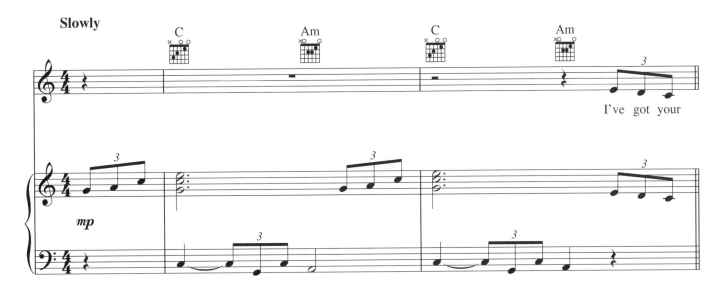

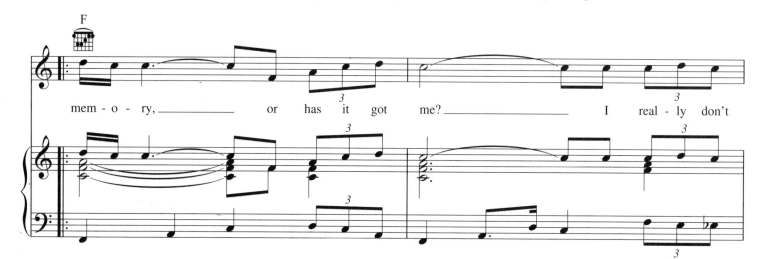

class ring _____ that _ proved you cared and it still looks the same ___ as when you

gave it, dear.___ The on - ly thing dif - f'rent, _____ the on - ly thing new, I've got these

lit - tle things, _____ she's got you. I've got your you.

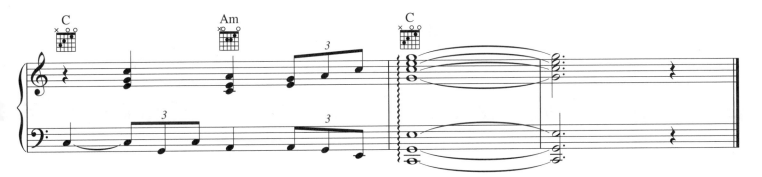

SOMETHING THAT WE DO

Words and Music by SKIP EWING
and CLINT BLACK

for-ev-er will ___ ring true. ___
and your weak - ness, too. ___

Love is cer - tain,
It's a lit - tle and a

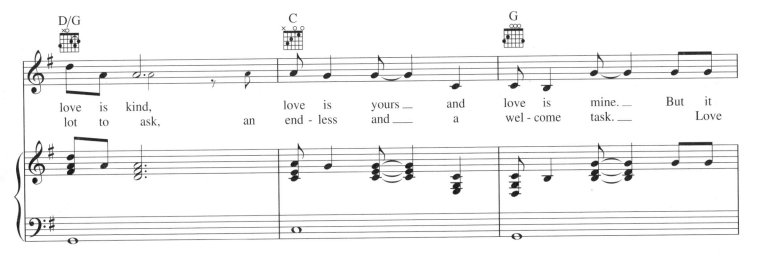

love is kind,
lot to ask,

love is yours ___ and
an end - less and ___

love is mine. ___ But it
a wel - come task. ___ Love

is - n't some - thing that ___ we find,
is - n't some - thing that ___ we have,

it's some - thing that ___ we do. ___
it's some - thing that ___ we do. ___

It's ___

We help ___ to make ___ each oth - er all ___

that we ___ can _____ be, _____ though we can find our strength and in-

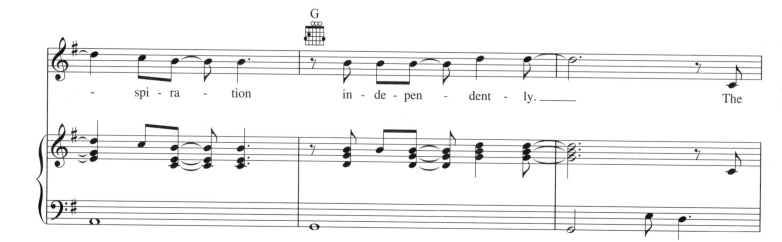

-spi - ra - tion in - de - pen - dent - ly. _____ The

way we work ___ to - geth - er is ___ what sets ___ our love ___ a - part, ___

_____ so close - ly that we can't ___ tell where I

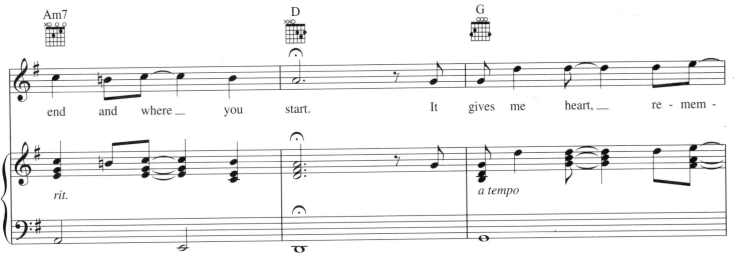

end and where __ you start. It gives me heart, __ re - mem -

- b'ring how __ we _____ start - ed with __ a sim - ple vow. __ There's __

__ so much to __ look back __ on now. __ Still it feels __ brand - new. __

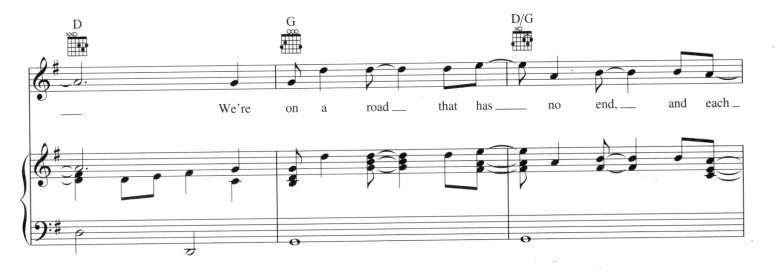

We're on a road __ that has __ no end, __ and each __

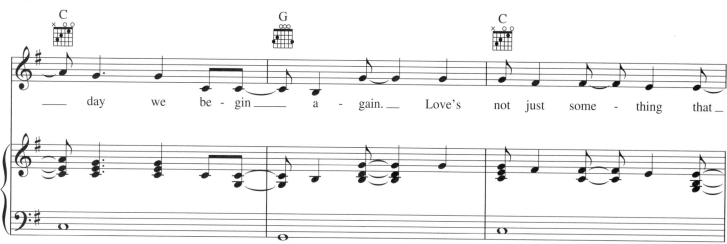

day we be-gin ___ a-gain. ___ Love's not just some - thing that ___

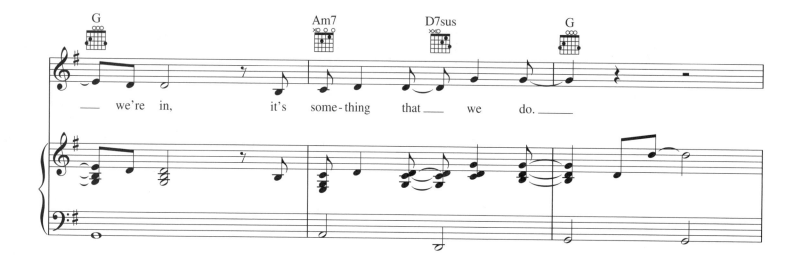

___ we're in, it's some-thing that ___ we do. ___

D.S. al Coda

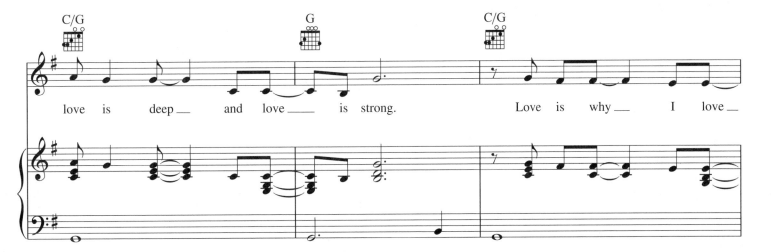

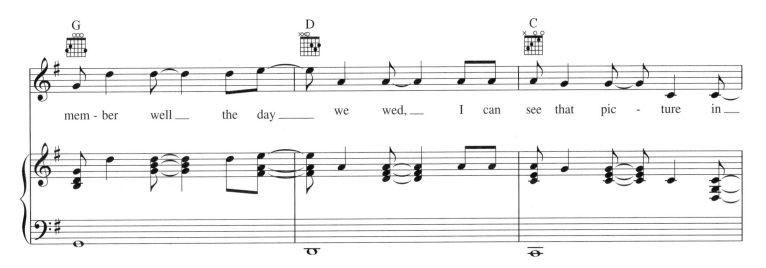

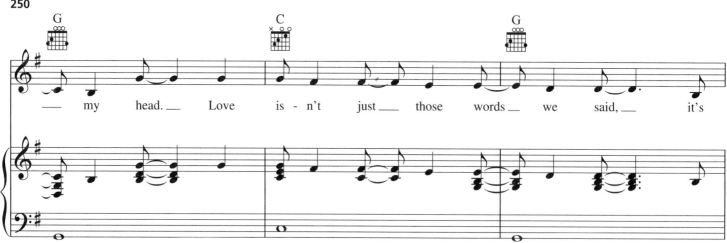

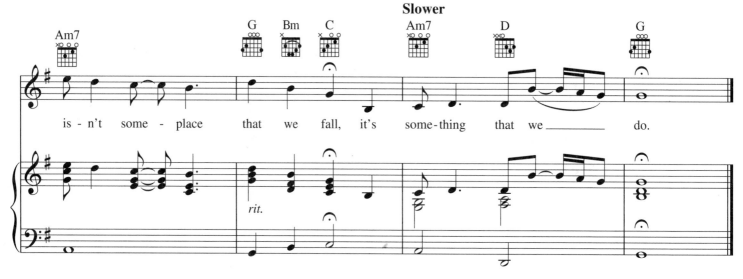

SWEET DREAMS

Words and Music by
DON GIBSON

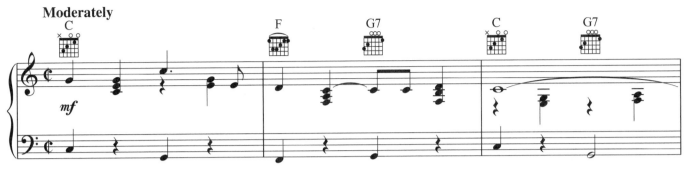

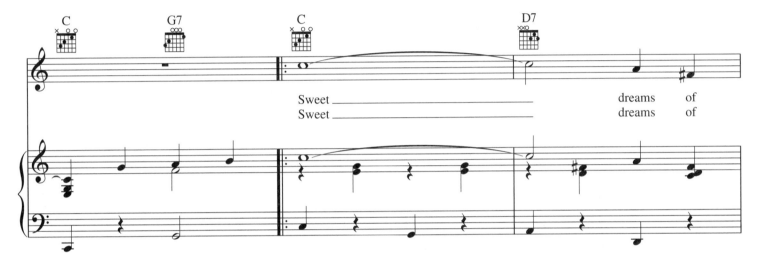

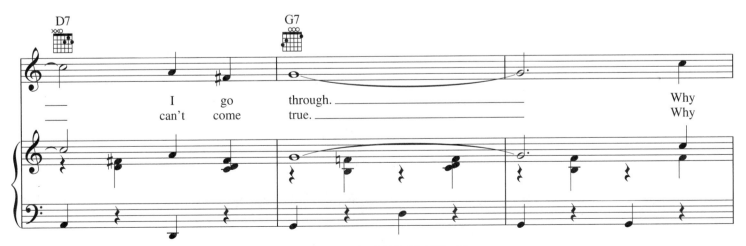

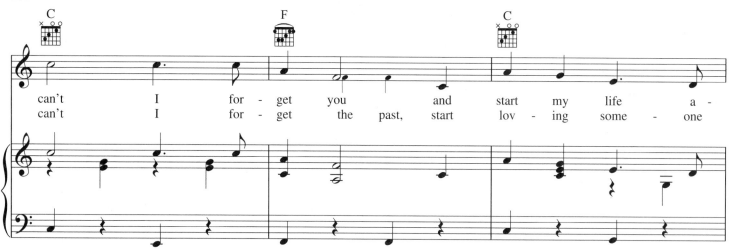

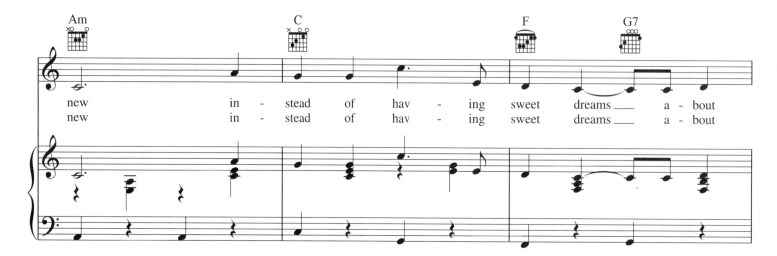

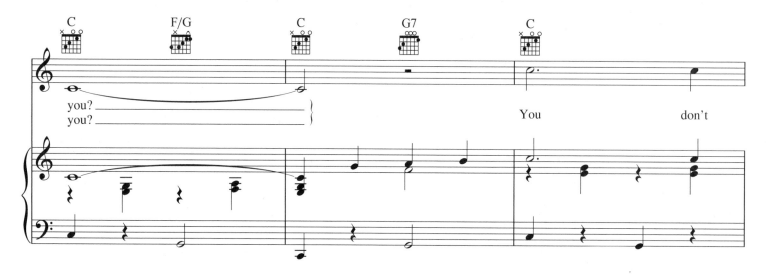

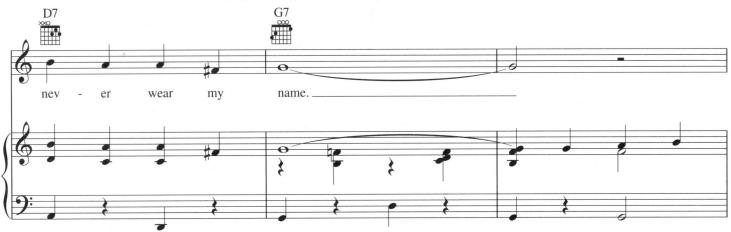

never wear my name. _____

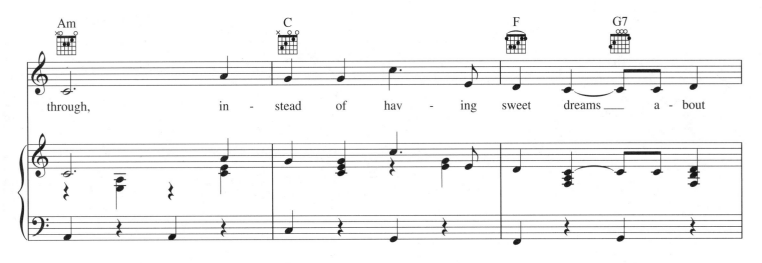

I should hate you the whole ____ night ____

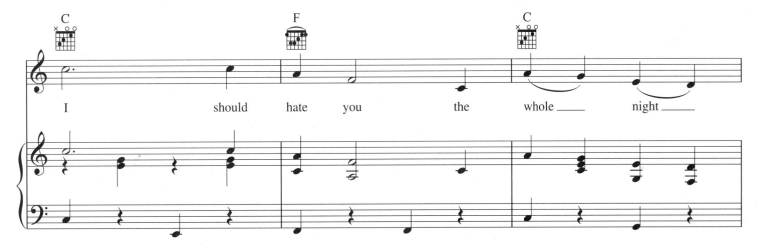

through, in - stead of hav - ing sweet dreams ____ a - bout

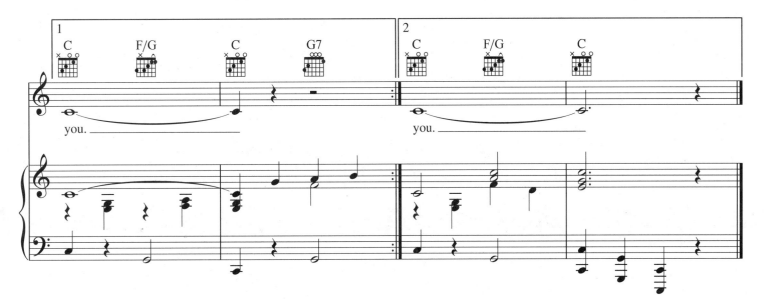

you. _____

you. _____

STAY FOREVER

Words and Music by HAL KETCHUM
and BENMONT TENCH

*Recorded a half step higher.

ev - er. ___ You don't have to go ___ on liv - ing ___

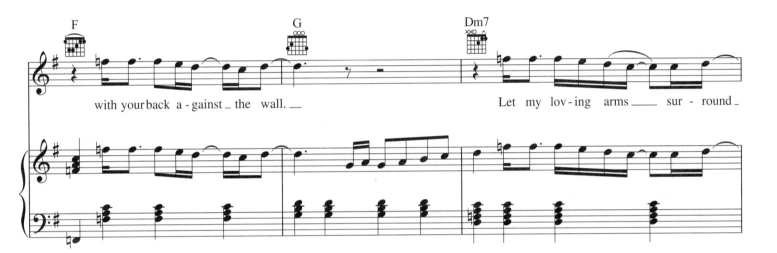

with your back a - gainst ___ the wall. ___ Let my lov - ing arms ___ sur - round ___

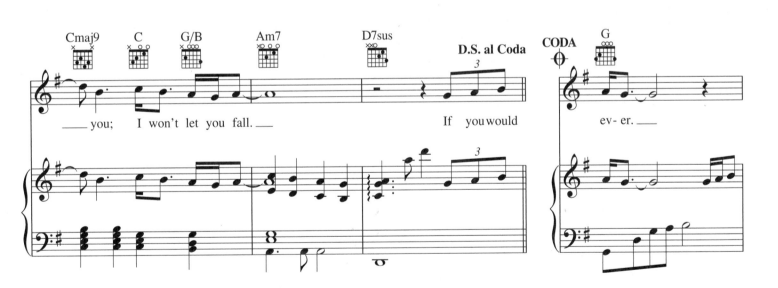

___ you; I won't let you fall. ___ If you would ev - er. ___

D.S. al Coda   **CODA**

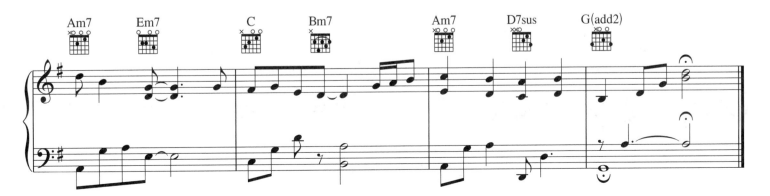

STILL

Words and Music by
BILL ANDERSON

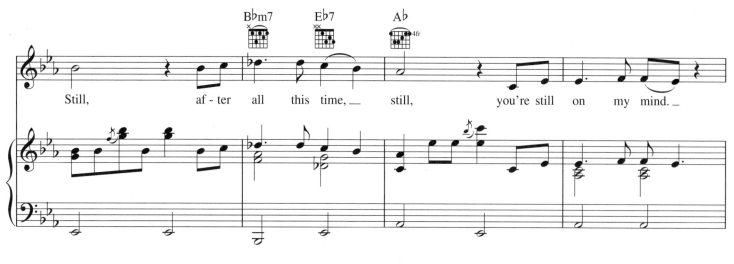

Still, af-ter all this time, _ still, you're still on my mind. _

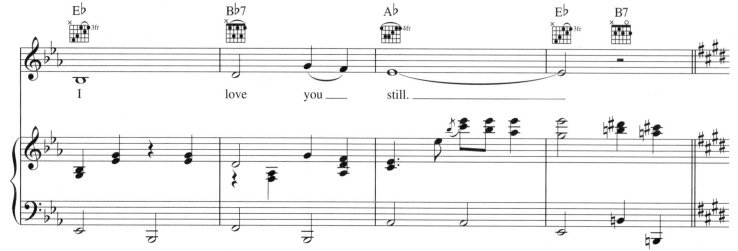

I love you _ still. _

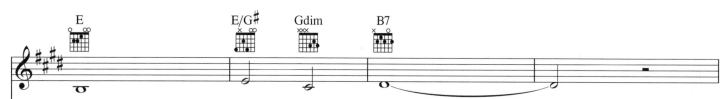

(Spoken:) This flame in my heart is like an eternal fire, for every day

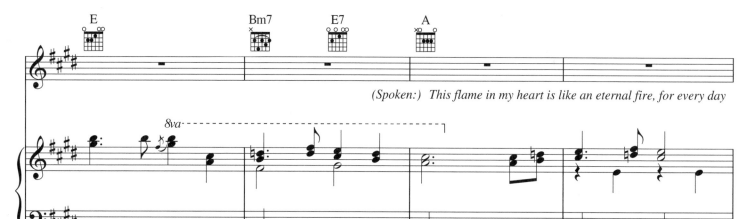

it burns hotter and every day it burns higher and I haven't been able to put out one little flicker, not even with all of these tears.
(Sung:) (I love you still.) _

THERE GOES MY EVERYTHING

Words and Music by
DALLAS FRAZIER

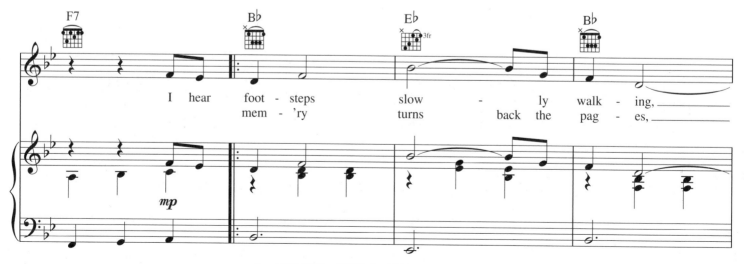

as they gen - tly walk a - cross _____ a lone - ly
I can see the hap - py years _____ we had be -

floor. _____ And a voice _____ is
fore. _____ Now the love _____ that

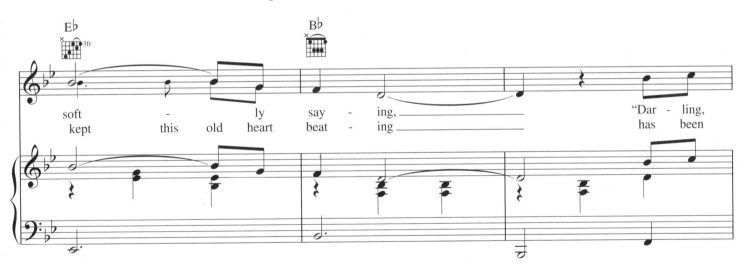

soft - ly say - ing, _____ "Dar - ling,
kept this old heart beat - ing _____ has been

this will be good - bye _____ for - ev - er - more." _____
shat - tered by the clos - ing of the door. _____

There goes my rea - son for

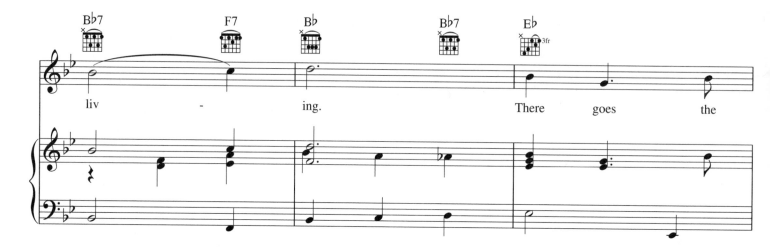

liv - ing. There goes the

one of my dreams.

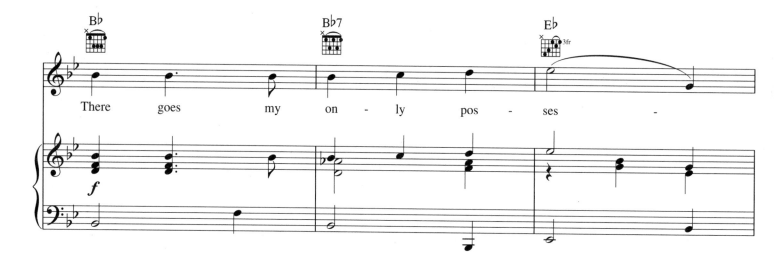

There goes my on - ly pos - ses -

sion.   There   goes   my   ev -   'ry -

thing.   As my thing.

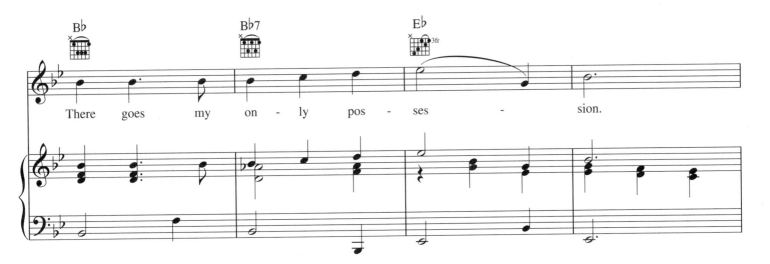

There   goes   my   on - ly   pos - ses   -   sion.

There   goes   my   ev - 'ry - thing._____

TILL I GET IT RIGHT

Words and Music by RED LANE
and LARRY HENLEY

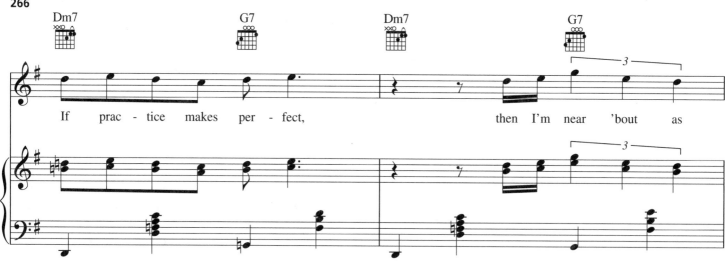

If prac - tice makes per - fect, then I'm near 'bout as

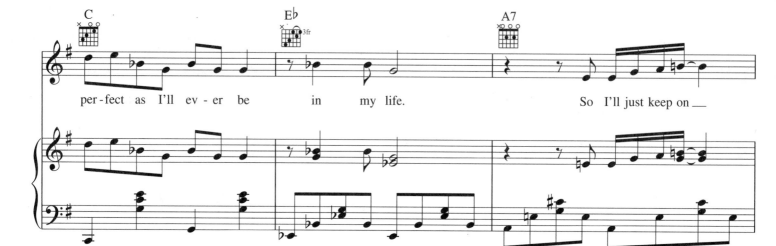

per - fect as I'll ev - er be in my life. So I'll just keep on __

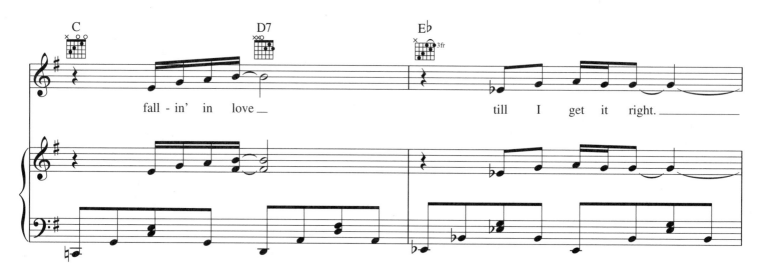

fall - in' in love __ till I get it right. _____

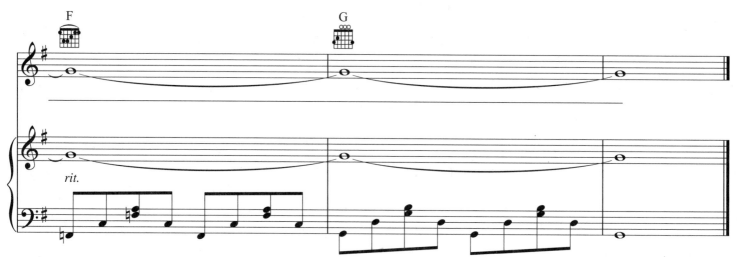

rit.

TILL THE RIVERS ALL RUN DRY

Words and Music by WAYLAND HOLYFIELD
and DON WILLIAMS

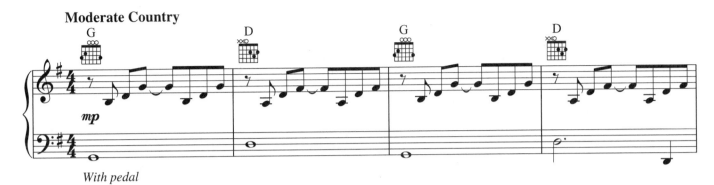

Till the riv - ers all run

dry, _____ till the sun falls from the

sky, _____ till life on earth is through, __

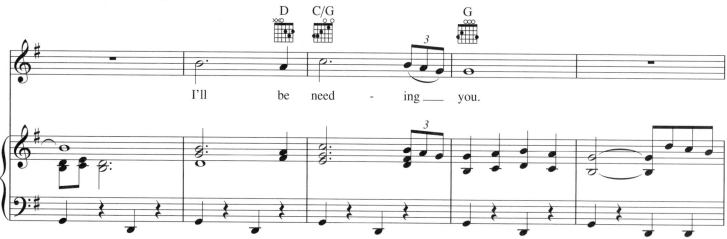

I'll be need - ing ___ you.

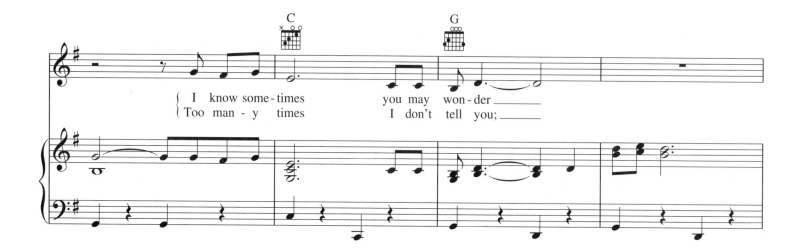

I know some - times ___ you may won - der _____
Too man - y times ___ I don't tell you; _____

from ___ lit - tle things ___ I say and do.
too ___ man - y things _____ get in the way.

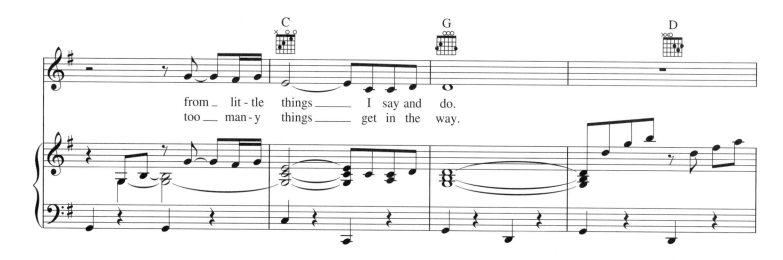

But there's no need ___ for you to won - der _____ if I
And e - ven though ___ some - times I hurt you, still, you

need you
show me

'cause I'll need you.
in ev - 'ry way.

Till the

riv - ers all run dry,
Instrumental

till the sun falls from the

sky,

till life on earth is through,

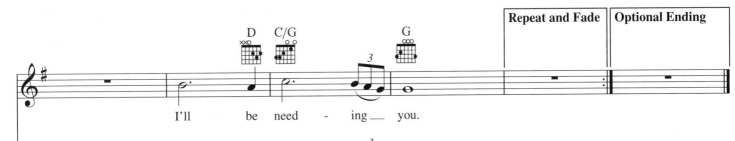

Repeat and Fade | **Optional Ending**

I'll be need - ing you.

TILL YOU LOVE ME

Words and Music by GARY BURR
and BOB DiPIERO

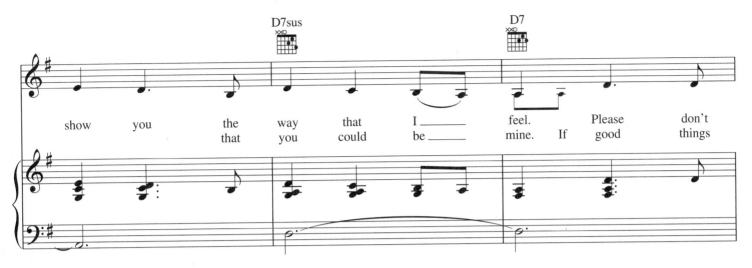

show you the way that I _____ feel. Please don't
that you that could be _____ mine. If good things

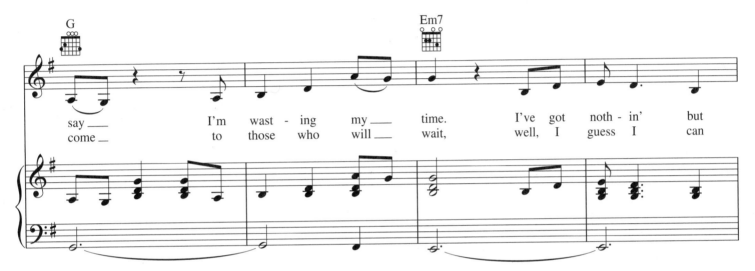

I'm wast - ing my _____ time. I've got noth - in' but
come _____ to those who will _____ wait, well, I guess I can

time, _____ so I'll do _____ all that I
wait, _____ if that's what I have to

can to catch that ghost of a chance. _____ The
do. Oh, it's worth it for you. _____

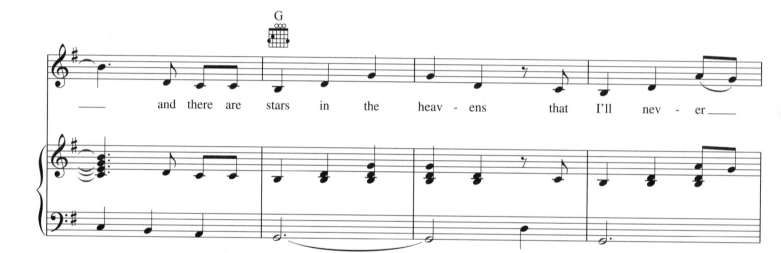

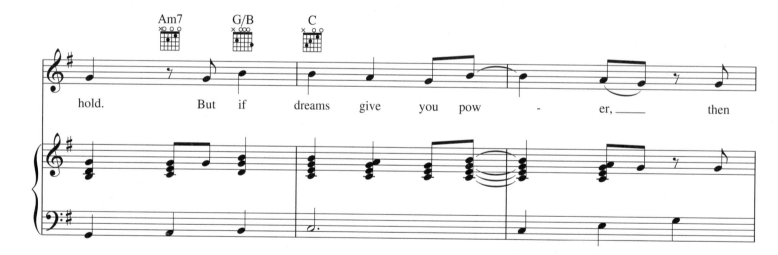

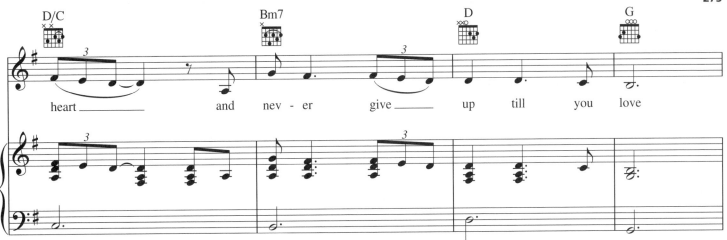

heart _____ and nev - er give _____ up till you love

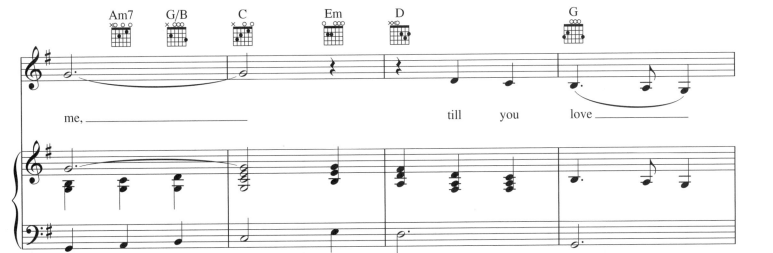

me, _____ till you love _____

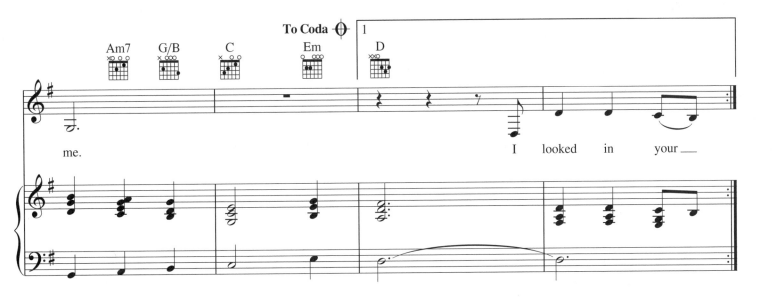

To Coda ⊕

me. I looked in your ___

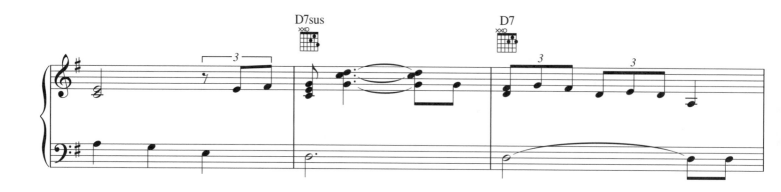

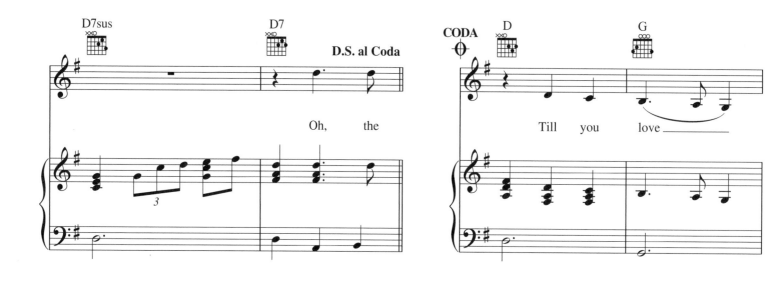

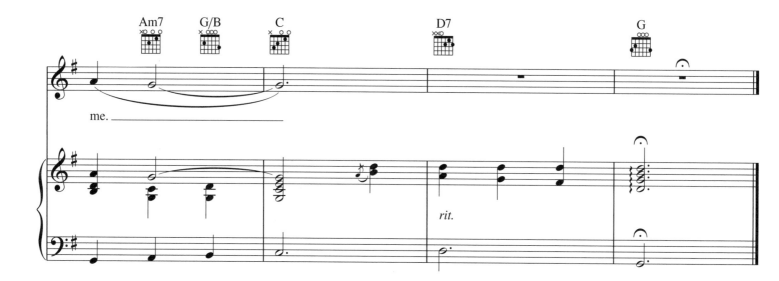

TIMBER I'M FALLING IN LOVE

Words and Music by
KOSTAS

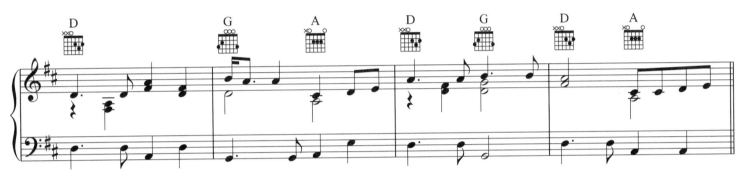

The right time, _____ the right place, _____ the right bod - y,
Who knows _____ how love starts. _____ I woke up _____ with _ you

the right face. _____ Tim - ber, I'm _____ fall - in' in
in my heart. _____ Tim - ber, I'm _____ fall - in' in

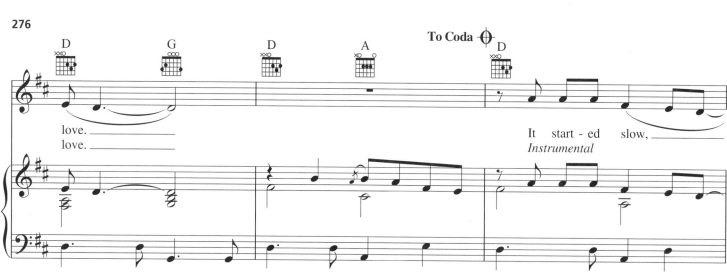

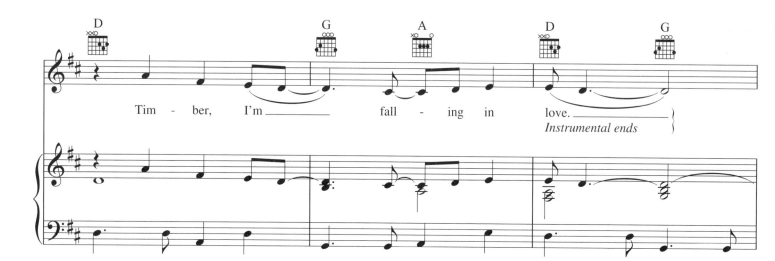

THE TIP OF MY FINGERS

Words and Music by
BILL ANDERSON

Moderately slow

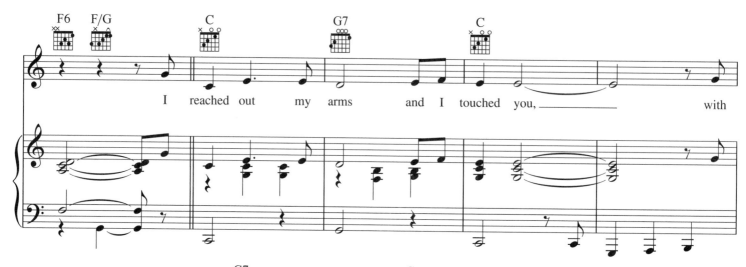

I reached out my arms and I touched you, _____ with

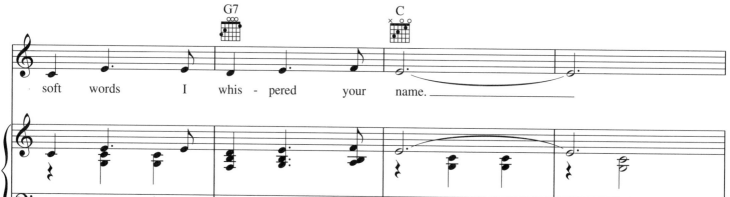

soft words I whis - pered your name. _____

I held you right on the tip of my fin - gers, ___ but

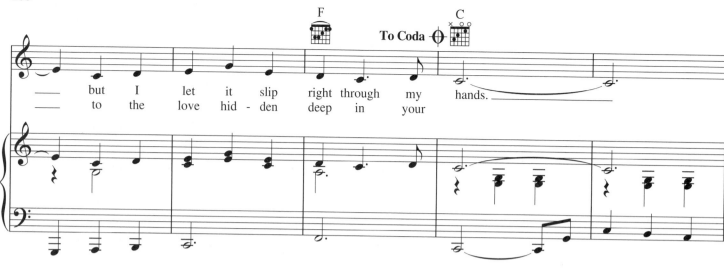

but I let it slip right through my hands. ____
to the love hid - den deep in my your

Some - bod - y took you when I was - n't look - ing ____ and

I should have known ____ from the start. ____ It's a

D.S. al Coda

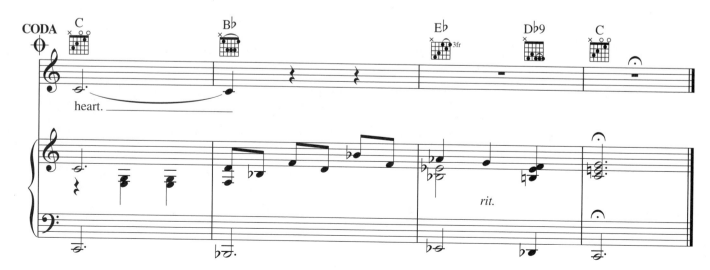

heart. ____

rit.

WE DANCED

Words and Music by BRAD PAISLEY
and CHRIS DuBOIS

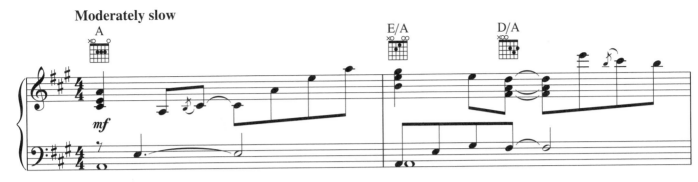

The bar was emp- -ty. I was ___ sweep-in' up the floor. ___

-ment there was ___ nev- er an- y doubt ___

That's when she walked ___ in. I said, "I'm sor- ry, but we're closed." ___ She said,

I had found the one ___ that I had al- ways dreamed a- bout. ___ And then one

"I ___ know, but I'm a-fraid I left ___ my purse." I said, "I
eve-nin' when she stopped by ___ af-ter work, ___ I

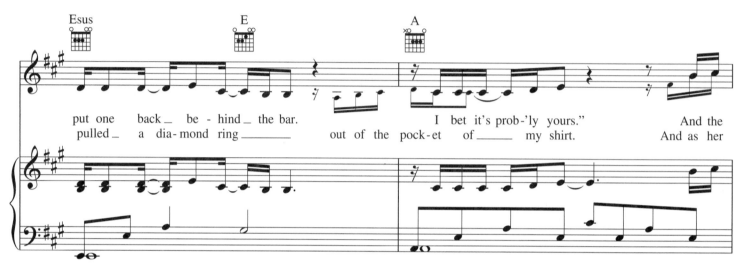

put one back ___ be-hind ___ the bar. I bet it's prob-'ly yours." And the
pulled ___ a dia-mond ring ___ out of the pock-et of ___ my shirt. And as her

next thing that I knew, ___ there we were ___ lost in ___ con-ver-
eyes filled up with tears, ___ she said, ___ "This is ___ the last ___ thing I ___ ex-pect-

sa - tion. Be-fore I
- ed." ___ And then she

hand - ed her her purse,
took me by the hand

I said, "You'll on - ly get this back on one con -
and said, "I'll on - ly mar - ry you on one con -

di - tion."
di - tion."

And we danced

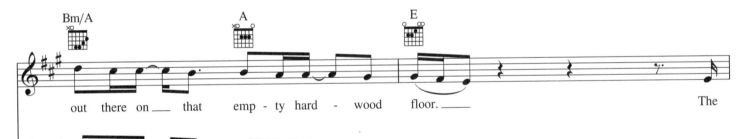

out there on that emp - ty hard - wood floor.

The

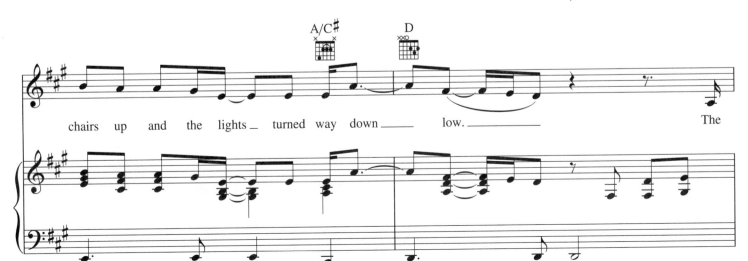

chairs up and the lights turned way down low.

The

mu - sic played, _ we held _ each oth - er close ___

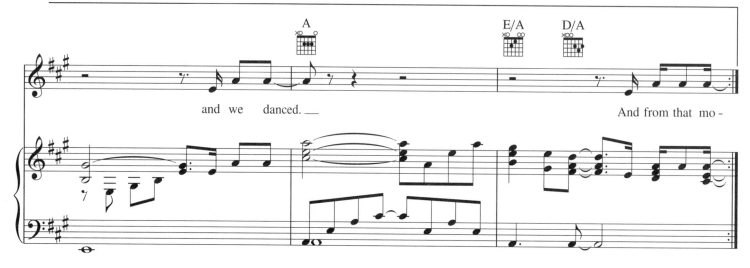

and we danced. _

And from that mo -

___ and we danced __

like

no one else had ev - er danced _ be - fore. ___

I

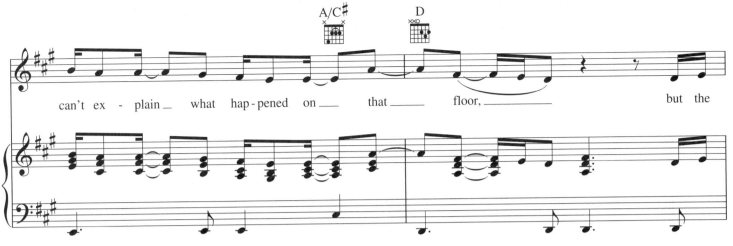

can't ex - plain _ what hap - pened on _ that _ floor, _____ but the

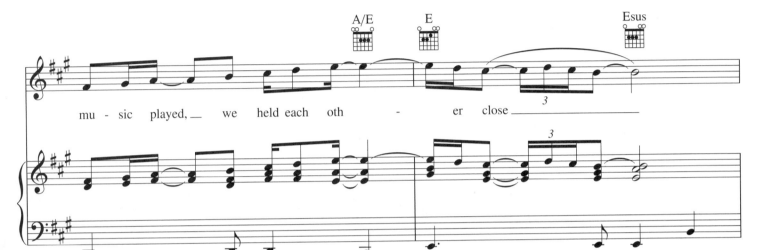

mu - sic played, _ we held each oth - er close _____

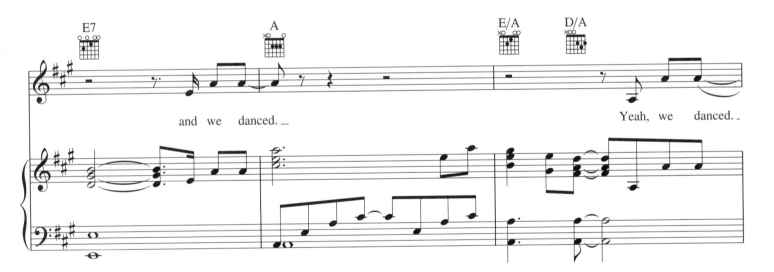

and we danced. _

Yeah, we danced. _

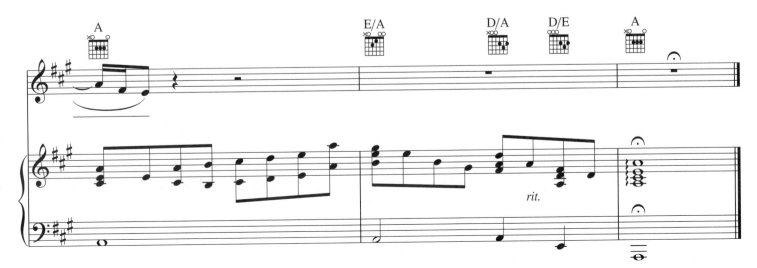

rit.

UNANSWERED PRAYERS

Words and Music by PAT ALGER,
LARRY BASTIAN and GARTH BROOKS

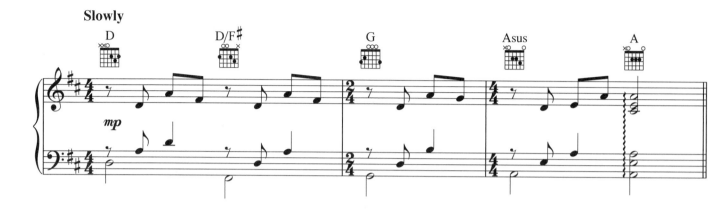

Just the oth-er night ___ at a home-town foot-ball game, ___ my
She was ___ the one ___ I want-ed for all times, ___ and
was-n't quite ___ the an-gel that I re-mem-bered in my dreams, ___ and

wife and I ___ ran in-to my old high ___ school flame. ___ And
each night I'd ___ spend pray-in' that God would make ___ her ___ mine. ___ And
I could tell ___ the time changed me, in her eyes ___ too, it seemed. ___ We

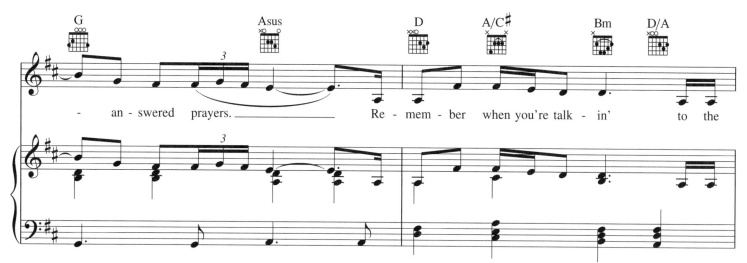

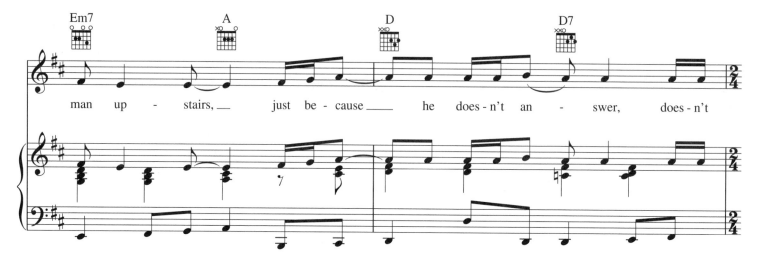

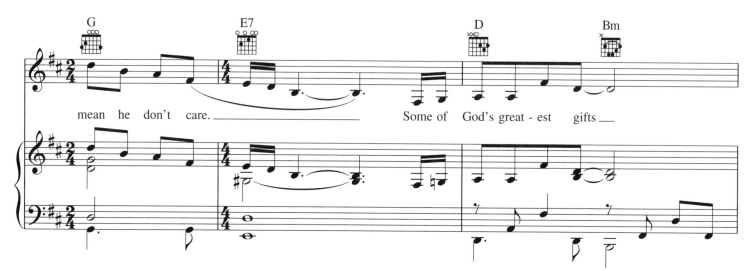

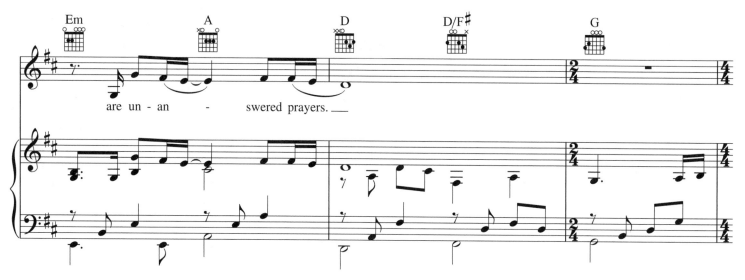

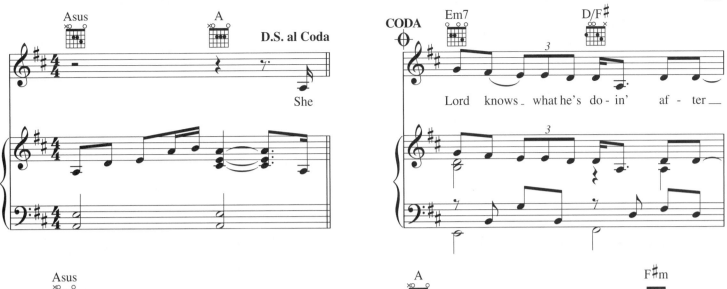

D.S. al Coda

She

CODA

Lord knows what he's do-in' af-ter

all. And

as she walked a-way, I looked at my wife, and then and

there I thanked the good Lord for the gifts in my life.

WELCOME TO MY WORLD

Words and Music by RAY WINKLER
and JOHN HATHCOCK

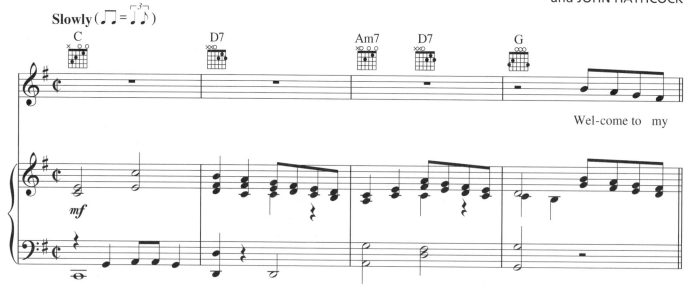

WHAT'S HE DOING IN MY WORLD

Words and Music by CARL BELEW,
EDDIE BUSH and BILLY JOE MOORE

What's he do-ing in my world? _____ What's he do-in' hold-in'

my world? _____ If he's not more than _ just a friend, then

why were you _ kiss-ing him? What's he do-ing in my world? _____

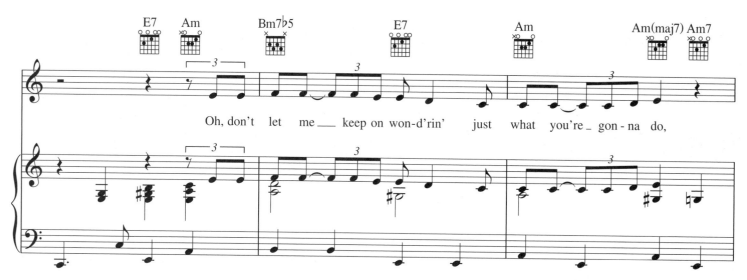

WHEN YOU SAY
NOTHING AT ALL

Words and Music by DON SCHLITZ
and PAUL OVERSTREET

Moderately slow

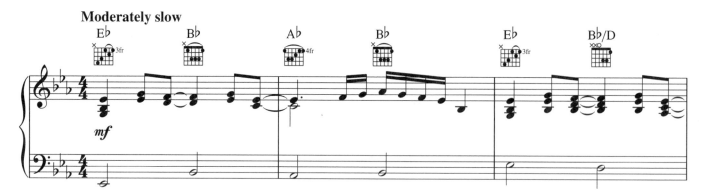

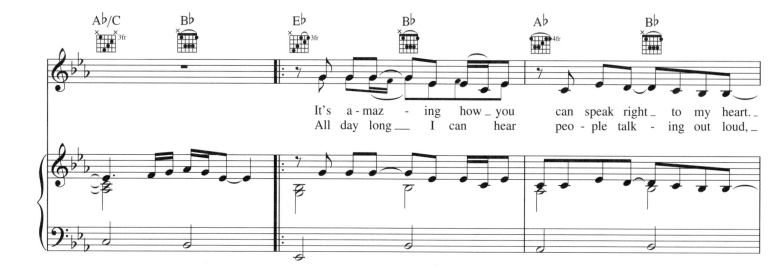

It's a-maz-ing how_ you can speak right_ to my heart.
All day long_ I can hear peo-ple talk-ing out loud,

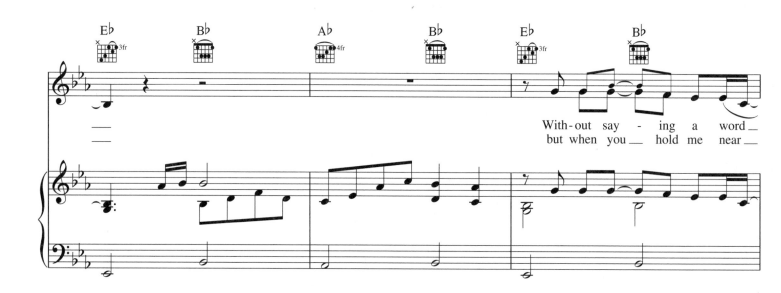

With-out say-ing a word_
but when you_ hold me near_

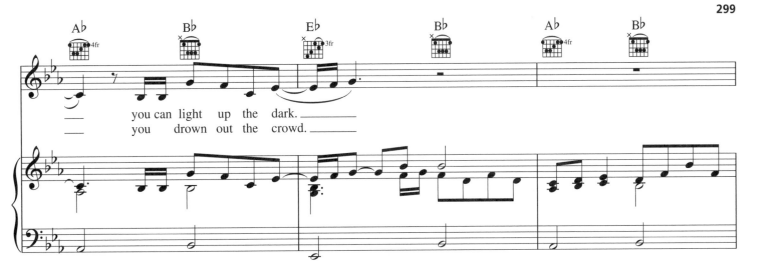

you can light up the dark. ____
you drown out the crowd. ____

Try as I may ____ I could nev - er ex - plain ____
Old Mis - ter Web - ster could nev - er de - fine ____

what I hear ____ when you don't ____ say a thing. ____
what's be - ing said ____ be - tween your ____ heart and mine. ____
The

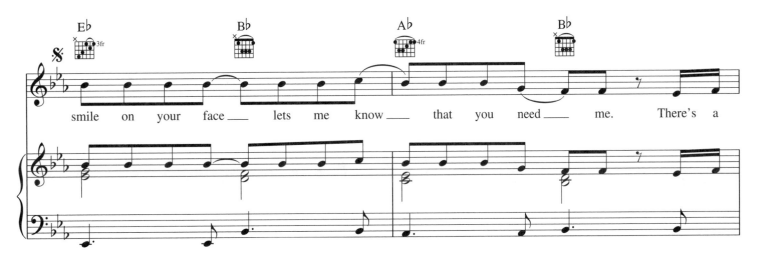

smile on your face ____ lets me know ____ that you need ____ me. There's a

truth in your eyes ___ say - ing you'll ___ nev - er leave ___ me. A

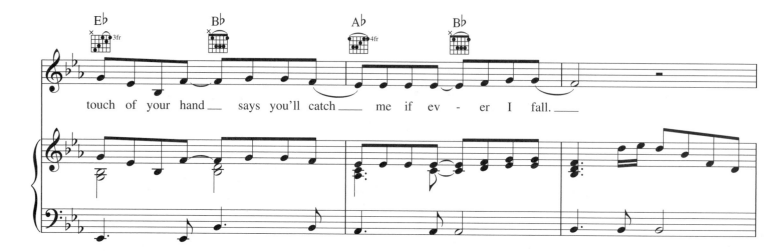

touch of your hand ___ says you'll catch ___ me if ev - er I fall. ___

Now you say it best ___ when you say noth - ing at all. ___

To Coda

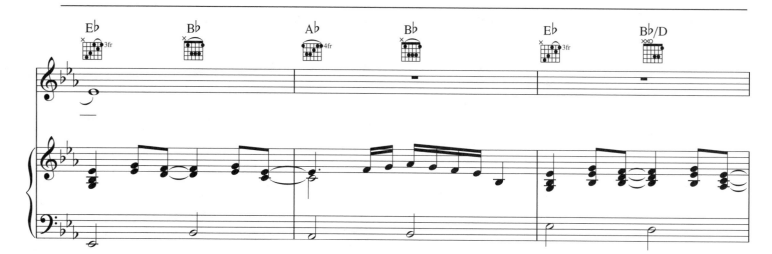

when you say noth-ing at all. _____

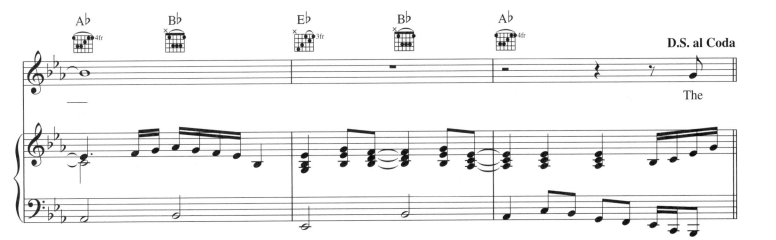

D.S. al Coda

The

CODA

when you say noth-ing at all. ____

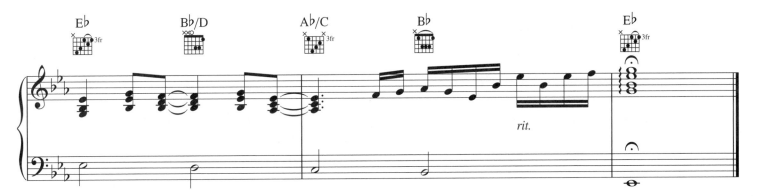

rit.

YOUR CHEATIN' HEART

Words and Music by
HANK WILLIAMS

Moderately

Lyrics:

Your cheat-in' heart will make you weep.
heart will pine some-day

You'll cry and cry and try to
and crave the love you threw a-

sleep. But sleep won't come
way. The time will come

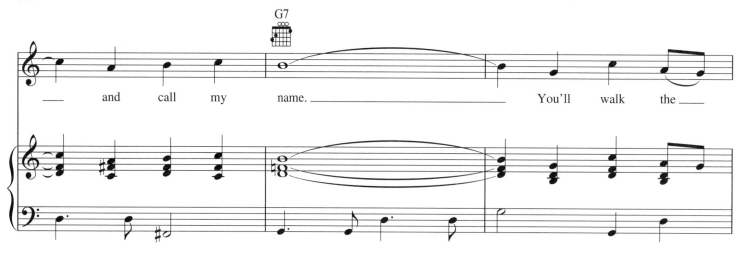

and call my name. You'll walk the

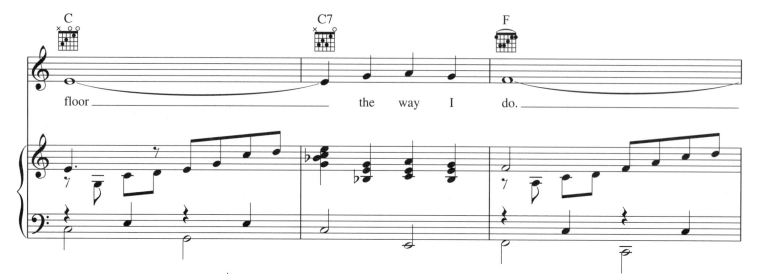

floor the way I do.

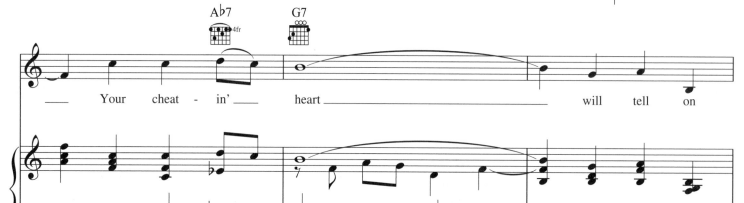

Your cheat - in' heart will tell on

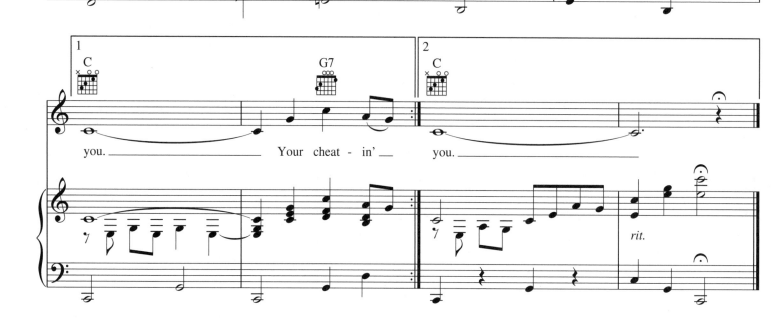

you. Your cheat - in' you.